THROUGH EYES OF FAITH

THROUGH EYES OF FAITH

CHRIS ELY

WINEPRESS WP PUBLISHING

ISBN 1-57921-124-0
Library of Congress Catalog Card Number: 98-60755

The purpose of this book is not to boast of any accomplishments I have made, for it is only through the constant support and encouragement of my family, teachers and friends that I have achieved. Rather, I write this to illustrate that individuals with disabilities can succeed and live productive lives in a world not fully prepared for them. It is my hope that it will serve as an encouragement to others with disabilities as well as all those without disabilities.

I wish to thank my parents, Charles and Annette, for their love and unselfish sacrifices in giving me every opportunity to go beyond what anyone thought possible. Special thanks to Billy Smith at West Texas A&M University for his contributions in editing this book.

All the glory goes to God, our Father, without whom I could do nothing.

Contents

First Steps

"You can do anything you set your mind to." Words that were planted firmly in my thinking from the time I was a small boy growing up in the flat, open country of West Texas. Mom and Dad embedded those words into my young, impressionable mind early. It didn't matter that I was different. If I tried hard enough, I could do anything.

My parents never set anything out of sight for me, even though I was born with a body I couldn't control. Growing up with cerebral palsy, I learned to work hard to get what came naturally for everybody else.

"You cannot do that" were words I never heard my parents say even though they knew there would be things I'd never get to do. They knew I'd never get to swim in the deep end of the pool. They knew I'd never get to chase a football. They weren't even sure if I'd ever walk, but they never kept me from trying. They only believed.

The day I took my first unbalanced step at 17 months, my parents were overjoyed. Mom ran to the telephone to call Grandmother Altman. "He did it! Chris can walk!"

she proudly announced. She called Grandma and Granddad Ely, Aunt Norma. She called everyone. She thanked God that I took that first step, convinced if I took one step, I'd take 100.

In time, I proved I could do things the doctors, my parents, and even I, never thought possible. It's because my parents had the faith to let me try despite all odds.

I saw what God made in me as part of a plan. I knew God had a purpose in everything, and everything that happened was part of God's plan for making me who I would become. God never promised an easy road, but he gave me the assurance that he would never leave me.

My family lived a quiet life in a small town in the Texas Panhandle. The Panhandle was about as far north as you could go and still be in Texas. It was a dull, uninteresting part of the country. Nothing but flatlands for miles in any direction. Sparsely spread trees and few hills or valleys, only the wind howling across the open fields.

Mom had lived in the sleepy, little town of Pampa, Texas, all her life. Annette was the oldest of four Altman girls. Grandmother and Granddad worked hard to send their children to school in long, frilly dresses with ruffles and lace that Grandma stitched by hand.

Money was scarce with four kids, and the family didn't have a lot. But they had a wealth of love. Mom was brought up in the old ways, taught to revere God and respect others. She knew the value of hard, honest work and tried to instill the same values in me.

Dad came to Texas as a boy. Granddad Ely brought the family to Pampa from Oklahoma when he worked for an oil company. They led a quiet, peaceful life, kept to themselves mostly.

They lived in a small house in a camp they shared with other oil workers just outside of town. Dad learned early on the value of a dollar and not to squander it on frivolous things.

Granddad bought a house and moved the family to town during Dad's last year in high school. My mother and father went to the same high school in the 1950s, but it was only after Dad returned from college and a stint in the Army that Annette met young Charles Ely.

A buddy of Dad's told him about the pretty, young girl working down at the electric company. He got up the courage to ask her out on Easter 1961. He took her to Caldwell's drive-in for a Coke on a sunny, Sunday afternoon. They dated weekends, while Dad worked at the ice plant in town. A year and a half later, they were married. They moved into a little house on Hamilton Street when my sister, Karen, was born a year and a half later.

It was situated in a quiet neighborhood, with a big back yard and a sagging Weeping Willow in the corner of the yard. It was a modest house, but love abounded in every tiny crevice.

I was a late comer into this world, about three weeks late to be exact. Mom and Dad had expected my arrival in early fall of 1968.

It was a joyous time for the new parents. Karen was nearly 3 and growing more every day. She was learning to take more steps and saying new words each day. Watching her sprout from a rosy-cheeked, wrinkly baby into a happy, healthy little girl, and now with a new baby on the way, my parents were filled with anticipation.

They weren't too worried that I didn't arrive right on time. After all, Karen was a late baby. It was natural, they thought.

Mom got up with expectancy every day, thinking, "Surely this would be the day." She made the painstaking effort of making sure she was dressed and ready to go to the hospital each day, despite the strain of getting clothes on in her frail condition.

The days and weeks passed until at last October came. Still, there was no sign of a baby. Finally, on a blustery day in late October, the time came.

Mom arrived at the hospital shortly before midnight. The nurses assured her there was plenty of time before the baby arrived. The doctor didn't even see my mother until the next morning. Mom always said if the doctor had only come to the hospital that night, things might have turned out different. If he had only come a little sooner . . .

Suspicions

When the doctor came into Mom's room before dawn
the next morning, he knew something was wrong
the minute he looked at her. The baby was in the wrong
position. They quickly began getting her ready and rushed
her to the delivery room.

I was born at 8:48 in the morning on October 19, 1968.
Mom was groggy when she came to, but she could hear the
doctor faintly in the distance. He was giving instructions
to the nurses, telling them to call another doctor. His
brother had a practice across the street from the hospital.

"Get him on the phone and tell him to get over here,"
he ordered the nurses. Mom, still queasy, could hear the
bustle in the delivery room. They whisked me off to the
nursery, while the doctor went out to talk to Dad.

He told him the umbilical cord had wrapped around
my neck, cutting off the oxygen to my brain for a short
time. There were no signs of injury to my body and brain,
but the doctor was unsure about the damage.

Dad's first reaction was fear. "Is there any brain damage?" Dad asked.

"He's down in the nursery; you can go and see for yourself," the doctor said sharply.

He assured Dad that I was all right. Truth was, he didn't know if I was all right. No one did.

Mom and Dad suspected something was wrong when they brought their new bundle of joy home from the hospital. As the days turned into weeks, and I began to grow, the bliss of having a new baby in the house quickly faded and their suspicions grew.

At five months, even though I was growing, I could not sit up on my own. A frantic call to the doctor brought a reassuring, "Don't worry." The doctor said some children develop slower than others, and that I would catch up.

My parents were frightened. Mom spent hours on her knees with tear-stained cheeks praying. She refused to let her fears make her faith grow weak. She believed I would be all right. I was showered with prayers. Grandmother Altman prayed. The church prayed. Mom even had the preacher say a prayer for me. He held me one Sunday morning and raised up my taut body and asked God to make me well.

My parents wanted to believe everything was going to be all right, but their hope was dwindling when at six months I was still unable to sit up alone. They propped pillows behind my back, in hopes that I would sit up on my own.

Grandmother Ely had noticed my slowness in development, too. One day, Mom had carried Karen and me over to Grandma's house. Grandmother Ely held me tightly in her arms and looked down at my clenched fists.

"There's something wrong with him," she said. "He can't straighten out his hands."

Mom tried to dismiss Grandmother's warning. "Your mother worries too much," she told Dad on the way home. By the time we got home, Mom was practically in tears. She couldn't help but remember Grandmother's words and wonder if she was right.

I showed little progress after nine months. I seemed alert and tried to sit up, but I lacked the balance to support myself.

One day, out of desperation, my parents sat me on the bed to see if I could sit by myself. I toppled over on the bed. Their hearts sank as they realized their greatest fears were true. It was obvious that something was not right.

More and more, my parents feared something was wrong. I wasn't crawling like a normal baby. I'd reach for a toy and drop it. I couldn't grasp a bottle to feed myself.

By my first birthday, Mom and Dad were frantic. All they had to do was look at me to know something was wrong. When Mom took me back to the doctor, she kept asking him if something was wrong.

He finally told them to take me to a specialist, hoping to relieve their growing fears. Mom and Dad made the appointment, praying for a miracle but fearing the worst. Either way, they had to know. They wouldn't be able to rest until they knew the truth.

Learning the Truth

I was a year old when my parents took me to a neurologist. The doctor only had to look at me to know what was wrong. He had seen it before.

After looking me over from head to toe, the doctor turned to my parents and told them frankly, "Your son has a nervous condition known as cerebral palsy."

Dad knew immediately what the doctor was telling them. He had heard of this crippling disease, and even seen others who had the disease. Mom, however, still didn't realize how serious my condition was. A tear streaked down Dad's cheek as he listened intently to the doctor.

The doctor said the condition was caused by a brain defect when the umbilical cord damaged the area of the brain that controls coordination and balance.

"How handicapped will he be?" Dad asked.

"He could live a happy, normal life or he could be severely disabled. Time will tell how severe the condition is and what he'll be able to do," the doctor told them.

The truth was out. Finally, my parents could admit to themselves that I would not grow up like a normal child. The question now was why. Mom was brought up to believe that anything was possible to those who have faith. Now, her faith was being tried.

My parents had prayed for a miracle. Had all their prayers gone unanswered? Mom wondered if she had done something wrong and now was having to pay for it — or that I was having to pay for something she had done. She couldn't understand why this was happening.

My parents shed many tears, but they knew they had to trust God and go on. It wasn't the answer they had hoped for, but God had given them an answer. My parents accepted my disability, and they were determined to do everything they could to give me a normal life.

They never gave up on me and never once looked back. My mother's prayers never ceased. She still believed a miracle was possible. Anything was possible.

They learned more about my disability in the weeks and months that followed. They started taking me to the Children's Rehabilitation Center for treatment.

The therapists exercised my stilted legs to strengthen the muscles. They stretched and bent my limbs like elastic bands, all in hopes my legs would become nimble enough that I would one day walk. The center's director said I probably would walk but would have a limp.

Physical therapists put me through my weekly dose of calisthenics, gently pushing and stretching my arms and legs, and they taught Mom to do the exercises at home. They offered encouraging words to my mother, telling her I probably would walk if my muscles became strong enough. It was a thought Mom held in her heart. I had to walk.

Mom and Dad diligently continued the exercises at home. They tackled the exercises with stringent determination. Morning, noon and evening, they put me through workouts. Mom practiced the exercises every morning, and Dad rubbed my legs with oil at night when he got home.

With patience and persistence, they followed this routine. They never gave up. I began to sit up on my own when I was 16 months old. I took my first unbalanced step a month later. It was the glimmer of hope my parents had waited for.

Other signs of growth followed slowly. The biggest obstacle was in learning to talk. Only garbled sounds poured from my mouth.

As soon as I showed signs of trying to talk, I was put under the close watch of Miss Appleby, a speech therapist at the Children's center. Miss Appleby was intent on starting the training early. She knew the importance of teaching a child early on to enunciate clearly, for she had the same malady as many of those whom she taught. She, too, had cerebral palsy.

At first, my parents were hesitant, even angry, that they would let someone like Miss Appleby treat me. "How could someone with a speech problem teach others?" Mom asked. They didn't understand, but after watching Miss Appleby, they saw that she had a better understanding than the most fluent speakers. They saw how determined she was to teach her students to speak clearly.

Her speech was affected slightly, though it was hardly noticeable by listening to her speak. Miss Appleby had worked hard to tame her tense, uncontrolled tongue. Her words were as distinct as a drill sergeant. She refused to let her words be slurred, and she demanded the same of her students.

When I got older, I got no sympathy from Miss Appleby when the words didn't come easily. She accepted no excuses for my mutterings. If I didn't say each word so she could understand it, she made me repeat it over and over after her. "You can do better," she said. "I know you can."

It took years before I could be easily understood. I could only say a few, simple words by 21 months, and they were only understandable to my family, but even then Miss Appleby tried to shape my speech patterns.

Speech therapy brought a whole new regimen of exercises for Mom and Dad to try at home. Miss Appleby told Mom to give me an empty bottle and let me start sucking on it.

It seemed like a mean trick to play on a little baby, but Miss Appleby insisted it would help loosen my tongue. It worked for a while, until I discovered the bottle was empty and refused to take it.

Miss Appleby tried more appetizing exercises as I got older. She spread peanut butter on a tongue depressor and positioned it at the top of my mouth. I had to swish my tongue to the roof of my mouth and sweep the peanut butter off the stick. It would get my tongue in the habit of naturally going to the top of my mouth when I made 'L' sounds.

I didn't mind the effort it took to wipe the stick clean. Sometimes, I got lucky and retrieved all of the sweet treat with one clean sweep, but usually it came off a little at a time.

After my speech lesson came my leg exercises. My walking had improved drastically by my second birthday. Mom would put me in my walker, and I'd take off scooting across the floor.

I was older than most children when I learned to walk, but the process was much the same. Dad stood a few feet away, coaching me to take those first unstable steps into his outstretched arms. Each week at the center, they worked to make my muscles limber, forcing me to stretch my legs.

My parents took the walker away when the seat broke. I cried for it at first, but after a couple of days I didn't miss it at all. After a few days, I was walking almost anywhere I wanted without support. From then on, it was all they could do to keep me out of everything.

The older I got, the more determined my parents were to treat me like any other child, showing no special treatment to me than to my sister, Karen. But each day they realized that we could not be raised in the same way. I was learning what I could not do; Karen was discovering all that she could do.

Mom and Dad spent time with both children equally, gave to both equally and scolded both equally. After spending all day at the center with me, Mom spent time alone with Karen at night. They played house, baking little cakes in a miniature oven. Or Mom would help Karen dress her dolls in new frocks.

Still, Karen had to realize that I took up more of Mom's time than she. It took more time to take care of me, more money for special shoes and more worries, but if Karen ever harbored a grudge against me, she never showed it.

She waited patiently while Mom was busy dressing me or as Dad gave me my exercises. As the older sister, Karen had a motherly touch and wanted to help Mom take care of me.

Karen was patient with me, even when I insisted on tagging along when she went out to play. She'd sometimes become angry when I burst into her room uninvited and would try to shove me down, but it was normal brother-and-sister strife. Karen never mistreated me.

If anything, I took my frustrations out on her. I was jealous because she got to do more than I did. I was left standing, staring out the front room picture window while Karen ran off to play with her friends. I wanted to be out in the middle of them, but I knew I couldn't.

"You might get hurt," Mom said. She was always afraid I'd get hurt among the romping of the other children.

Karen sometimes took me with her when she went out to play, even though I often slowed her down. It was hard for her to watch all the neighborhood children run and play and not be able to go with them because she had to watch after me.

I was furious when she left me behind. I would try to scream at her, but my tongue would get tied in knots and I wouldn't be able to get the words out.

I was left all alone and had no one to play with me. There was no one to pull me in the little, red wagon that I loved so much.

I was enraged when Karen left me. I went into her room when she wasn't there and threw her things around the room. I wanted to be like the other children. I couldn't stand it that my clumsy feet wouldn't carry me everywhere I wanted.

My parents saw my frustrations. They surprised me with a shiny new tricycle on my fourth birthday. It was purple and had brightly colored streamers dangling from the handlebars. The neighborhood children laughed at it because they all had two-wheelers, but to me it was the best bike on the block.

Even though Dad wouldn't let me take it past the neighbor's driveway, I found a new freedom. Now, I could keep up with the other children. At last, I was one of them.

True Test

If I was slower learning to walk and developing physically, my parents were afraid I would be slower at learning mentally, too. The doctors comforted them by assuring them the area of my brain needed for learning remained unscathed. They believed I could learn the same as any other child.

My aunt ran a school for retarded children, and she suggested that my parents have me tested to be in her school. Aunt Ruth was a boisterous and plainspoken woman. She shared the same unyielding faith as my mother. She encouraged my mom in the days after I was diagnosed with cerebral palsy.

Aunt Ruth urged Mom to bring me to the sheltered workshop, where she taught mentally retarded and handicapped children. She said it could only help me to get out among other children and have playmates my own age. There, at least, I could get training to live a normal, independent life.

Mom and Dad were uneasy about taking me to a school for the mentally handicapped. Like all parents, they wanted to believe their little boy was a little smarter than any other child. They hoped, at least, I would go to regular school.

Still, they had to consider the possibility that I might not be able to attend school with regular children, so one afternoon Mom took me to visit Aunt Ruth's school.

From the outside, the school was impressive. It was in a beautiful old church. Lush, green lawns stretched across the landscape under the shade of beautiful old trees. The inside told a different story.

A sea of far-off stares met us. I clenched Mom's hand tightly as we walked around the room. The older children greeted us with broad smiles and proudly led us across the room to the projects they were working on. Many of them were more handicapped than I was. They were sitting in wheelchairs and strollers. Many didn't talk as well as I did; some not at all.

Mom's eyes became moist with tears as she looked around the room, hoping she wouldn't have to leave me in that place. Aunt Ruth encouraged her, saying if I came to the school, she could work with me and teach me to read and write and do all the things normal children do. Her words were little consolation, however, to a mother who hoped her child would attend regular classes. But my parents agreed to an IQ test.

A few weeks later, they took me to the State Center for Mental Health and Mental Retardation in Amarillo for an intelligence test. Mom took great pains getting me ready for my evaluation. She dressed me in a brand-new jumpsuit and warned me to do exactly what the doctor said. Both she and Dad were intent on making a good impression on the doctor.

The psychologist watched as I played with the toys in the small office. The tests requiring the use of my hands — counting out small, wooden blocks or placing tiny pegs in holes — were impossible. I sent the blocks flying off the table and across the room when I tried.

The doctor went on to the psychological tests. Mom always said I had a remarkable memory. I could count to 10 and recite Aunt Norma's telephone number from memory by the time I was 4. The doctor seemed impressed when I repeated a series of numbers back to her without hesitation.

The psychologist sat scribbling on a note pad as Mom and Dad waited patiently. They were relieved when the tests were over and they could take me home. The tests concluded I had average intelligence and that my disability was not severe enough to require special schooling.

My parents were quite relieved. Now, they could concentrate on getting me ready for school — regular school.

My birthday fell late, so I couldn't start kindergarten with the other children when I turned 5. I had to wait until the fall, almost a full year after all the other kids started school. Still, Mom and Dad wanted me to learn so I didn't fall too far behind.

Dad arranged to get me in Head Start kindergarten. My parents thought it would give me that extra boost to get me ready to start regular school. It helped that Dad was a schoolteacher and knew the right people to talk to to get me in the program.

I was glad when I started to school. I had watched Karen head off to school every day, and I wanted to go, too. I'd ask Mom, "When can I go to school?"

"You'll go someday," she said. "Someday."

When I finally started to Head Start kindergarten, I was excited. I knew the sacrifices that had been made to get me in school. Even at an early age, I knew I was different from other children, so I knew it was a miracle that I was even there.

From the first day, I was treated as any other student. The class was small and methods of teaching advanced. A small cluster of caring teachers and aides catered to each student's needs to give him that extra boost.

All the mothers took turns coming to school to help with crafts or storytelling. Mom came to class once a week. She helped with crafts and went with us on field trips. I loved when Mom came. I clung to her and wouldn't let her out of my sight.

She also came every day at mealtime. I couldn't feed myself without making a mess of the floor and myself, so Mom came and fed me my lunch. Mealtime was an ordeal at home. Mom thought I should be feeding myself. She tried to get me to rely less on her help and more on using my ability to help myself, but I refused to cooperate.

I tried to feed myself, but it was too hard. Once I got a bite on the spoon and hoisted it up to my mouth, the spoon would tip over and I would spill the contents. It would be so much easier if I could pick up the food with my hands and stuff it in my mouth. I used my hands until Mom told me I had to be neater with my food.

She put the spoon back in my hand and told me to try again. I fought her every step of the way. Finally, she'd say, "All right, I'm going to give you a bite, then you're going to get a bite," hoping that I would at least take a few bites on my own. It went back and forth. Mom would feed me a bite, then I would force a small morsel onto the spoon and edge it up to my mouth.

We stayed at the dinner table long after everyone else had finished — until every bite was cleared from my plate.

Mom had a tender heart, and it hurt her to see me struggle, so at school she gave in and did it for me. She didn't want to start a fight, and it was just easier that way.

It was different at school. I cooperated with my teachers. I was expected to do all the things the other children did, even coloring and writing. I didn't argue with the teachers when they gave me an order. I just did it.

The hardest thing was learning to print my name. My hands shook so that my writing was almost illegible. With a tight grip on my thick pencil and perspiration pouring down my forehead, I tensed my arm so it wouldn't shake when I wrote. Soon, I began to show progress and learned to print my first name.

I made many new playmates at school. The other children saw that I was different, and they were naturally curious about me. Most were nice to me, but some were cruel. I'd see them point at me and ask their parents why I walked funny.

The parents, rather than try to explain that I was handicapped, just told them to hush. "It's not nice to stare," they would say. They wouldn't tell them why I was different, so many grew up not knowing about the handicapped. They didn't know that I was just like them in many ways.

They saw me as that poor crippled boy whom they should pity. Many carried their prejudices through life and never took the time to get to know me.

I was content to stay at school, except when Mom came to class. Mom made the mistake of letting me go home with her one day, and from then on I wanted to go with her every time.

Mom came to school one day, and I begged to go home with her. We were going to the cafeteria, and I started begging to go with her. She told me I couldn't go with her, but I kept on. I started crying and screaming. I threw a fit in front of the whole class, but Mom didn't give in this time and insisted that I stay at school.

I threw such a tantrum that Mom just had to walk away and leave me. I yelled all the louder, but she kept walking.

Mom was never quite sure what to do with me when I had one of my outbursts. Wanting to be a good mother but still learning how to raise a handicapped child, she was afraid to be too harsh with me, but she couldn't give in to me every time I had a tantrum either.

It wasn't the first time I had raised such a ruckus. One day, Mom took me with her to the grocery store. I loved to get in the basket as she pushed me around the store. As we passed the toy aisle, I spotted a little truck on the shelf and begged to get down and play with it.

"Only for a few minutes," Mom said. "Then, we have to finish our shopping."

I made zooming sounds as I scampered up and down the aisle pushing the truck. Round and round it went. I loved watching the little truck. Finally, Mom was ready to go.

"Put the truck back now. We have to go." But I wasn't ready to leave yet. I kept pushing the truck.

"We have to go now," she said, taking the truck and putting it back on the shelf. I let out an earsplitting squeal and started bawling. People started peeking around the corner to see what was happening. Mom was terribly embarrassed that her son was behaving that way. There was nothing she could do to get me to quiet down. I was howling.

Finally, she picked me up and carried me screaming from the store. She had to take me home to Dad, then go back and get her groceries.

The next week when we went to the center, Mom asked the director, Mr. Balke, if she had done the right thing or if she should have given in to my tantrum and let me play with the truck.

Mr. Balke assured her she had handled the situation as any good mother would. "It's bad to have a child who's handicapped, but it's worse to have a child who's handicapped *and* spoiled," he told her.

Mom learned that if she didn't discipline me I would be completely unbearable. From then on, she made it clear that "no" meant "no," and when she told me I had to stay at school, I had to learn to do as she said.

As the year went on, I made some progress in learning. Even the Head Start teacher said I was advanced for my age, and by the end of the year, they felt I was ready to start regular kindergarten.

Mom and Dad were proud of each accomplishment I made, no matter how small. When I wrote my name for the first time, the letters were barely distinguishable because my writing was so shaky. Still, they raved over it. They took nothing for granted because they knew each accomplishment came at a price.

School Days

I had no fears about starting kindergarten the next fall despite being forced out of my safety zone of Head Start, where the pressure to compete was lessened. I was thrust in among 25 able-bodied children who could run and play freely with no thought to trying to keep their balance.

Kindergarten saw many firsts. Not only was it a new experience for me, it was a first for the teacher, too. It was Mrs. Gross's first year to teach, her first day in the classroom, and I had been foisted upon her. She must have been terrified. No training for becoming a teacher could have prepared her for that day. Mrs. Gross never had been taught how to work with a student with a disability.

Mrs. Gross was kind and patient and did her best to help the other children understand and educate herself about my disability.

We all learned a lot those first few weeks. I knew I wasn't like the other children. Like ducks in a row, I sat alongside my classmates on mats in the floor while Mrs. Gross read the class a story. I gazed strangely around the room at the other children, and I saw that I was different. It felt strange being with them, like I shouldn't even be there.

Growing up with cerebral palsy, I knew there would be things I couldn't do. Like running and chasing after the other kids in a game of freeze tag or ducking a speeding ball in dodge ball. I couldn't join in their games, so I had to be content to watch.

I sat at the side of the playground and watched the sports. I was quick to chase any runaway balls that came my way and toss them back onto the court. Like the others, I raced for the swings and fought for a turn on the slide, even though I often lagged behind the rest of the group. If I got too far behind, one of my classmates ran back and grabbed my arm, and with a gentle tug, would lead me to the rest of the class.

Sometimes, just climbing the steps to go into the building was a struggle, but the children lined up to help. They all wanted to help me when I needed it.

I took tumbles as I fought to keep my balance on my wobbly feet. I wore a helmet to soften the landing when I fell. The helmet was quite strange looking. It looked like the headgear of an early football team. A chin strap kept the helmet firmly planted on my head, and a soft, thin padding lined the inside. It protected my head from the knocks and bumps I took every day. But it also brought some curious stares.

The first time our principal, Mr. Jones, saw me wearing it, he asked, "What in the world has that kid got on his head?"

The teacher explained that I had to wear it because I lost my balance and fell a lot.

At first, he felt sorry for me. He would see me coming down the hall. He'd watch until I passed and just shake his head. So did a lot of other people when they saw me for the first time. They wanted to help, but they didn't know how.

It didn't take long to see why I needed the helmet. One trip through the halls usually would end with a spill.

When I did fall, everyone rushed over to see if I was all right and to help me up. Everyone except for one boy in the class. Derrick Smith. Derrick was sort of a self-appointed bodyguard. He'd see the kids all milling around me in the hall, and he would push his way through the crowd.

"Leave him alone," he would tell the others.

Then, he'd come over to me and say something like, "Quit lying in the floor, Chris. You're holding up traffic. Get up from there."

People who didn't know thought he was being mean, but Derrick knew that's how I wanted to be treated. The last thing I wanted was people feeling sorry for me. "You won't get anywhere from people feeling sorry for you all the time," Mom and Dad always told me. I had to make it on my own.

With an outstretched hand, Derrick would reach down and pull me to my feet. Sometimes, I got only a few feet before I fell again. To make things worse, I wore leg braces. They were called twisters because they turned my feet outward to help me walk straight.

I wore them on the inside of my pant legs. A strap fastened around my waist, and the braces ran down my pant legs and attached to my shoes.

I had hightop shoes. They were heavy and made quite a clatter when I walked down the hall. Clip-clopping down the hall in my hightop shoes and braces, a helmet planted on my head, I was quite a sight.

The extra weight of the shoes pulled me down. It usually didn't hurt anything except my ego when I fell because

I had trained myself how to fall. After many bumps and bruises on the noggin, I learned to keep my head up when I took a tumble. And the helmet helped to soften the blow.

Of course, Derrick was always there, too, if I needed help. He was always there to gently pick me up.

"You put another hole in the floor?" he'd quip. Then, he'd lift me up, and I would be on my way again. The rest of the class hurried on ahead, but Derrick stayed with me until I got where I was going.

I lagged behind the others, partly because of my heavy shoes, but the delay wasn't entirely because of my feet.

The teachers knew it took me longer, so Derrick and I dallied in the hall. We lingered in the hall as long as we could — or as long as we could get by with. If we stayed too long, though, the teacher came looking for us.

"Chris fell again," Derrick would tell her. "We're coming."

As the year went by, I made still more progress. I was getting used to being away from home all day and felt more sure of taking care of myself. I started to do more for myself and lost some of my self-consciousness over being around the other children. I wanted to do more things myself. I wanted to be independent.

Mom still came to class occasionally, but I was learning to make it on my own. Of course, Mom was thrilled that I was becoming more independent, but she had to learn to let go.

One day, we had an assembly, and all the students had to carry their chairs to the gym. Mom was going to carry mine, but I didn't want help. I wanted to carry the chair along with my classmates.

"No! I can do it," I told her.

I pushed her away because I was determined to carry the chair. And I did. Mom had to let go and let me try to make it on my own. But she was right there if I needed help.

Growing Pains

Mom never stopped believing in God's ability to give me a normal life. Even though she didn't understand why I should be afflicted by this thorn in the flesh, Mom never lost faith. Her prayers never ceased even as I got older. She carried me to prayer meeting after prayer meeting, hoping against hope that I would be healed.

From the time I was old enough to understand, my parents taught me to call on God to help me. Mom took my sister and me to church every Sunday. She did her best to help me understand my disability.

Mom said I must not be bitter about it, but to accept it and trust God to help me. I couldn't understand why I was the way I was. I was taught to look to God when I had questions.

Mom and Dad tried to give me a normal life, even though there were things about me that were anything but normal. Mom dressed me for school every day. She saw to it that my shirt was buttoned straight, my pants were snapped and my shoes tied before I left home. It's hard enough for a first-grader to learn to tie a shoe or button a button, but for someone with cerebral palsy, it seemed impossible.

I simply couldn't make my tense hands wind those shoe-strings around into a neat little bow, so Mom had to tie my shoes for me.

At school, I didn't want to ask anyone for help. I wanted to make it on my own. I tried to wait until I got home to go to the bathroom. At home when I had to go, Mom or Dad would unfasten my pants, then I could go on and use the bathroom.

One day, I had an emergency at school. I had to go to the bathroom. I waited as long as I could, but I had to go.

I raised my hand and asked to be excused. Derrick usually went with me to help me or there was someone in the bathroom who could help me. But that day, there was no one else in the restroom.

I unbuckled my belt without much problem, but I couldn't get the snap loosened. It was the kind of hook that I had to slide over to get it undone. I struggled with it for several minutes, but I couldn't get it loose. By then, I really had to go. I was working with it when . . . it was too late. I wet my pants.

I was so embarrassed. I was afraid to go back to class. Everyone would laugh at me. I quickly got some paper towels and tried to dry the wet spot, but it was no use.

I went back to the room and slid behind my desk. It was about an hour until school let out. I had a jacket at my desk, so I put it over my lap hoping I could hide the stain.

At the end of the day, Mrs. Burns, my first-grade teacher, always picked someone to help her pass out papers. I usually liked to pass out the papers, but that day I prayed she wouldn't call on me. I sat at my desk, praying the bell would ring before she chose someone.

"Chris, would you hand out the papers for me?" Mrs. Burns asked.

I couldn't hand out the papers. Everyone would see what I had done, I thought to myself.

I got up, trying to keep the jacket over the wet spot. By then, Mrs. Burns had noticed what had happened. She called me to her desk. "Didn't you make it to the bathroom?" she asked.

I explained to her what happened. Mrs. Burns had compassion on me. She didn't embarrass me. She quietly led me into the hall and helped me get dried off before anyone noticed what had happened. "Next time, if you need help, let me know. I'll get someone to help you," she said.

I waited in the hall until the bell rang. No one ever knew what happened, not even Mom. Mrs. Burns said it would be our secret. I never forgot her kindness to me that day.

I left school early one day a week, and Mom took me to the Children's center for treatment. Besides speech and physical therapy, I went to occupational therapy, where I learned to rely on my own abilities to do the chores of everyday living.

One room at the center was arranged like a kitchen, where I practiced feeding myself. Another was a bedroom, with a bed, dresser and a large mirror. The third room was a bathroom, and the fourth a workshop. Miss Connie took me to one of the rooms each week for my lesson.

The weeks when we went to the kitchen were met with great anticipation. I loved the trips to the kitchen because I got to eat. But I was filled with anxiety the weeks she would lead me into the bedroom or the bathroom to practice dressing.

Connie had a block of wood with a piece of cloth on it. The cloth was tacked to the sides of the board and had buttons in the middle.

She showed me how to put the button in the buttonhole, then it was my turn. Even though they were the size of silver dollars, I could not make my stiff hands grab hold of one of the buttons and get it to go through the hole. I would just get the button in the hole when my hand would slip and the button would fall out.

Connie sat patiently, encouraging me to keep trying.

I was convinced I'd never button a shirt. It seemed so impossible. How could I manage the tiny buttons on a shirt when I couldn't manage the giant ones? I had no desire to button a shirt, so I refused to even try. I quit. I didn't want it bad enough.

Mom felt sorry for me. I was relieved when she laid out a pullover shirt for me to wear to the center, so I wouldn't have to practice buttoning it. Still, Connie made me practice pulling the shirt on and off over my head.

I stood in front of the over-sized mirror and practiced taking off my shirt and putting it on again. I had little trouble getting it off, just slip it over my head. The hard part came when I tried to get my arms back in the right holes and get it over my head.

Connie used a stopwatch to track my progress. I had to keep doing it until I could get my shirt on in under three minutes. Once, I stuck my arms in the wrong holes and got the shirt on backward. Connie made me take it off and start again. I was furious. I didn't want to try again. "I CAN'T!" I demanded.

"You can, and you will," Connie said.

I gained speed as the weeks went on. By the time we finished, I could take my shirt off and put it on again in less than three minutes.

Socks were another seemingly impossible feat. Trying to stretch the sock wide enough to get my foot through was just too much to handle.

I'd try to get my foot in the hole but miss the hole. Sometimes, I'd get my foot in the sock and start to pull it up, when my hand would shake and the sock fell off. My temper flared. I'd throw the sock across the room and run find Mom. I came to put my socks on in record time, but it wasn't without much practice and determination.

I refused to even try to tie my shoes. I had convinced myself I couldn't do it. My stiff fingers got in the way when I tried. Instead of tying knots in my shoestrings, it was usually my fingers that got tied in knots.

Connie tried telling me if I couldn't tie my shoes I'd never really have the independence I wanted so desperately to achieve. I would always be depending on someone else.

But Connie wasn't going to force me to do something I didn't want to do. Unlike Mom, Connie wouldn't fight me to get me to learn. I had to want to learn, and I already had my mind made up that I couldn't learn. So, I just gave up. I didn't try.

That decision will haunt me for the rest of my life. Years later, when I got out on my own, I had to humble myself and ask for help when I needed my shoes tied because I didn't try when I was young. Even though I bought shoes that had no shoestrings to tie, I had to live with my decision. I had to admit failure over something as little as a shoestring.

I often regretted that I didn't try harder when I was young. I lost part of my independence because I didn't learn to do more for myself. I resigned myself to just getting by and did not try. Mom and Dad tried to instill in me the value of hard work. "You can do anything if you try," Dad badgered me.

But by the time I was 8 years old, I was still as helpless as a baby around my parents. I wanted them to do everything for me. I tested my parents to see how much I could get them to do for me.

I was at the age when I should have been dressing and feeding myself, but I still depended on Mom to do it for me. She put my socks on me in the morning and tied my shoes. She cut up my food and even spoon-fed me.

Dad was not taken in by my helpless act. "You'll learn to feed yourself or you'll go without," he said. He wasn't being mean. He just wanted me to learn, but I'd run to Mom, hoping she would have pity on me.

I could do more than I let on, but I was lazy. It was easier if Mom did it, and she was so good-hearted it was hard for her to say no. But even she had her limits.

"I'm not always going to be here to do these things for you," she'd say. "You need to learn to do it for yourself."

But I would keep on until she'd finally get tired of arguing with me and just do it. I wanted her to do everything for me, even help me with my bath.

I was nearly 9 years old, the age when most boys would shutter at the thought of their mothers seeing them naked! But I was not embarrassed or ashamed to ask her to help me.

"I might fall," I said to try to earn her sympathy. I had lots of excuses. And it was just easier if she did it.

I was in the bathtub one night, and Mom, under duress, was helping me with my bath. While I was in the tub, though, Mom told me she was *not* going to keep bathing me and that I was going to have to start dressing myself.

"I can't!" I declared. "You have to help me!"

"You're too old for me to keep giving you a bath," she insisted.

By the time the bath was over, Mom was all upset and I was in tears. But she had made one thing clear — she wasn't going to help me get dressed. She lifted me out of the tub and started drying me off.

"Will you help me get dressed?" I asked.

"No. You're going to have to put your clothes on yourself," she said.

"Please!" I begged her.

"I'm sorry, Chris, but I'm not going to do it for you anymore."

I started screaming. Finally, she just had to leave the room. I yelled for her to come back, but she ignored me.

"I NEED YOU TO HELP ME!" I yelled.

After about 10 minutes of this, Dad had heard enough. "Where's the belt?" he shouted from the living room.

I was standing in the doorway, stark naked, when I heard him starting toward my room. I hurried over to the chest and grabbed my clothes out of the drawer and started pulling them on. But by then it was too late.

Dad turned me across the bed and laid into me. He gave me a sound spanking.

"Your mother is not going to do it for you. Understand me?"

I nodded a forlorn "yes."

I cried into my pillow that night, partly because of the blistering, but more for feeling sorry for myself. Why didn't my parents see that it was easier to have everything done for me? Deep down, I knew they were right. I knew I was only hurting myself.

My malingering didn't end when I got to school. Although I had made progress, I was content to merely pass from grade to grade. I didn't put forth my best effort. School was like a playground for me, a place where I went to see my friends and have fun. I didn't take it as seriously as I ought. I was content simply to get by.

When the teacher assigned class work, I would sit at my desk and pretend to study. Many times, I would be doodling or gazing out the window. I didn't try to learn.

In third grade, the teacher assigned a slate of vocabulary words each week and had the class write each one 10 times. I couldn't see any sense in this. It was a strain just to write the words once, and she wanted me to write each one 10 times?

My pencil scrawls were almost illegible, and it took me longer to write out the words than the other students. I just couldn't see any sense in it, so I made up my mind I wasn't going to do it.

The first week I didn't turn in a paper, the teacher told me I would have to make it up if I hoped to get a passing grade in spelling. After several weeks, she became concerned because it wasn't just spelling I had fallen behind in. I had put off other assignments, too — in reading and math.

One week, we had a substitute teacher, and I didn't turn in any homework. The substitute thought that because I was disabled, maybe I was excused from written assignments. But my classmates quickly told her different.

I fell further and further behind, and I found new excuses for not having my work. Finally, the teacher called me up to her desk. Stumbling to my feet, I began the long walk toward the front of the classroom.

Tears streaking down my cheeks, I faced my teacher and pleaded that I be allowed to make up the work. The teacher looked at me for a minute and said, "Chris, you're getting further behind." She told me I might have to repeat the third grade.

The thought of repeating the third grade sent a streak of terror up my spine. Out of desperation, I vowed to turn in every assignment from then on. The teacher scribbled out a note and told me to take it home to my parents.

I knew if I showed the note to my parents I would get a spanking for sure. All my parents asked of my sister and me is that we did our best and worked hard. They wouldn't tolerate such laziness.

I couldn't take the note home. When the class went to recess that day, I stood off to the side by myself. Then, when no one was looking, I hid the note in a cement slab that was overgrown in weeds. No one will find it there, I assured myself.

When school let out, I went home relieved that I had spared my backside a sound spanking. That was Friday afternoon. By Friday night, I started to worry.

What if someone finds the note? I'll really be in trouble then, I told myself.

My conscience began to bother me a little, too. That night, I had a nightmare that someone found the note. I was miserable the whole weekend. All I did was worry about the note. By the time Monday morning arrived, I couldn't wait to get to school. I was up and dressed for school early. I had to get that note before someone found it!

When Mom dropped me off at school, I immediately went to the playground and to the old slab where I had hid the note. I ruffled through the tall weeds and grass until — there it was. I could see it. I grabbed the note and headed for the building.

I wrapped the note in another piece of paper and dropped the bundle in the trash can in the hall. I wasn't worried that someone might find it in the trash. I guess I thought once they emptied the trash, it would just disappear.

I took heed to the teacher's warning. I turned in my spelling words that week and every week after that. I vowed to become a model student. I feared that I'd have to repeat third grade.

I lugged books home every night, enlisting the willing help of Mom and Dad in going over and over my homework. I began studying the minute I got home in the afternoon and did not rest until my homework was finished.

I began to apply myself more than I had in the past. I learned that when I did my best and applied myself, I could always succeed.

Valuable Resources

Watching my progress, my parents were even more determined that I should overcome my handicap. At the end of my third-grade year when they met with the teacher, school counselors and therapists, they decided to place me in a resource class for an hour each day.

Most of the students in the resource room weren't physically disabled, but instead had learning disabilities and needed a little extra attention. I was placed in the resource room for motor development. A teacher gave me exercises to loosen my poorly coordinated hands and give me more dexterity in my hands and arms.

I loved going to the resource room because, for one thing, I got to leave class for an hour every day. I also was enamored by the resource teacher, Miss Stuart.

She had flowing locks of golden curls. I thought she was far too beautiful to be a teacher. I liked to sit and stare at her. Schoolboy crush scarcely conveys the doglike devotion I had for Miss Stuart.

I could hardly wait for her to come get me out of class each afternoon and take me next door to the resource room. We spent a whole hour some days working a puzzle together. Another day, she had me stacking little blocks, shuffling them from one side of the table to the other. Miss Stuart praised each move with words of encouragement.

"You're doing so well," she would say.

At the time, I failed to realize how patronizing it all was. I was so thrilled by her attention and kindness, I was blind to what she was really doing. How hard is it to stack blocks?

It wasn't that Miss Stuart meant to patronize me, or any of the resource students for that matter. It's just that she didn't expect any more from us. But then, I didn't expect any more out of myself.

I started in the resource room late in the year, so I was in the class only about six weeks before school was out for the summer. When school began again in the fall and I went back to the resource room, I was heartbroken to find that Miss Stuart was no longer there.

Instead, I found my former kindergarten teacher, Mrs. Gross. And although I didn't know it at the time, that would be the year everything started changing.

Mrs. Gross wasn't content to let me play for an hour. I was going to have to work that year. Her job was to get me to apply myself physically, and this was no easy task.

One reason it was called a resource room is that teachers often had to scrounge for learning material. The only thing they had for motor development were the toy blocks and a Nerf ball, and Mrs. Gross said she wasn't going to waste her time and mine throwing a Nerf ball to me for an hour each day.

I came along before there were computers in every classroom. All they had when I entered the fourth grade was an
old Underwood typewriter that Mrs. Gross found in the
teachers' work room. She borrowed it, and it was conve-
niently left in her classroom for me to use.

Mrs. Gross thought a typewriter was ideal for developing motor skills because I had to have coordination to use
the typewriter keys, so she set out to teach me to type.

I learned my own technique on the typewriter. My
hands lacked the dexterity to use all my fingers to type. I
started out using one finger, my thumb, and a rather crude
hunt-and-peck method. I soon discovered the thumb wasn't
the best suited for typing and switched to my index finger.

It was slow-going at first. It took me practically the
entire hour to type a single page from a book, but as I learned
the keyboard, I picked up speed. Mrs. Gross arranged for
me to do my spelling on the typewriter. In the fourth grade,
we still had to write our spelling words 10 times, but typing them made it easier.

It took less effort to type the words than it did to handwrite them. The typewriter became my second set of hands.
Mom and Dad were thrilled that I was learning to type, and
they got me an old typewriter to use at home.

I typed all of my homework instead of handwriting it. I
stopped dreading assignments because it took less effort,
physically, to type my homework. My grades also improved.

It was then that I started developing an interest in writing. I wrote stories about my family on the typewriter in
Mrs. Gross's classroom. The first story I wrote was about
my dog, Snoopy.

Everyone had been telling my parents that Karen and I
needed a dog. Even Mrs. Gross suggested that a dog would

be good company for me. So, after much persuasion and promising to be good from then on, Mom and Dad agreed to get us a dog.

When we got him, he became part of the family right away. He was a little white poodle. He looked like a little rat when we brought him home. Snoopy seemed to find his way into just about everything. When he was a puppy, he got into the clothes hamper while I was at school and chewed holes in my socks. I wrote a story about it in the resource room the next day. Mrs. Gross liked it and encouraged me to write more.

I used the old typewriter my parents bought me to write stories about Mom, Dad and Karen. It wasn't exactly elegant prose, but it was something I enjoyed and something that I seemed to be good at. Before that, I hadn't found anything that I was genuinely good at.

Typing opened a new world to me. I had all these thoughts in my head, but because of my difficulty in talking I would give up and not talk because people simply didn't understand me. I became frustrated when people couldn't understand me, so I wouldn't try to talk.

Typing changed that. I found a way to express the words that I had kept locked inside my head. It was a way to communicate when the words didn't come easily. Teachers would tell me, "Don't talk. Type it," if they couldn't understand me.

I started typing everything. It was easier and faster than writing, and it allowed me to get the words out. It also boosted my weak ego, and my grades improved because I was typing all my homework.

My life was changed because someone believed in me and took the time to make a difference. Mrs. Gross saw past my disability to my ability. She focused on what I could do, not what I couldn't do, and she worked to bring it out. That made the difference for me, and it was all because someone cared.

Summer Camp

Summer can last an eternity when you're young. Each day became a new adventure in frivolity and frolics. The trees came alive and spring turned to summer. The days grew longer and the sun was out longer, warming the hard ground that had been frozen all winter.

It was a carefree time filled with the things that kids love — a day at the swimming pool, splashing in the cool water; a game of tag with neighborhood kids; and summer camp.

I wanted to go to camp like my friends. Mom and Dad sheltered me as a child. They wanted to protect me from the harsh world and were afraid to let me go out on my own because I still couldn't do some things for myself.

They were reluctant to let me go away from home because I relied so much on them. So for one week each summer, the neighborhood was deserted while all the kids went off to camp. Except for me.

Every year, I begged them to let me go and every year they said the same thing, "How could you make it at camp when you can't do things for yourself at home?"

The spring before my 11th birthday, I heard the kids at the center talk about a camp for handicapped children. I made up my mind that, one way or another, I was going to go to camp.

I started working on Mom first, softening her up to ask her if I could go. I knew if I wanted my parents to let me go I had to prove I could make it away from home. I started doing everything for myself — as much as I could anyway.

Miss Connie and the therapists at the center tried to convince Mom and Dad that two weeks away from home would do me good. I would have to learn to survive without them.

I hinted about camp every week when we went to the center. Then, on the way home one day, I came out and asked them if I could go. They didn't answer me right away. They just said, "Well, we'll think about it."

They didn't say no, so at least I still had a chance. Mom and Dad still weren't convinced I could make it away from home, but they agreed to think about it — on one condition. I was going to have to be more independent. That meant feeding myself and dressing myself. All the things I relied on Mom to help me with, I would have to do myself at camp.

Connie assured Mom that camp counselors would help me if I needed help, so Mom and Dad finally consented to let me go.

The Lions Club sponsored the camp for disabled children. Local clubs raised money to send kids to the camp in Kerrville, Texas. It started the week after school was out in June and lasted two weeks.

The weeks leading up to camp were filled with a flurry of activity. Mom hustled around the house sewing name tags in all my clothes and gathering up enough clothes to last me two weeks. I could hardly believe I was actually going.

Kerrville was some 500 miles from where we lived in the Texas Panhandle. Mr. Hicks was a member of the Pampa Lions' organization, and he agreed to drive me and a girl from Pampa, Alisa Burns, to Kerrville.

I could hardly sleep the night before we left. I woke up a half-dozen times during the night, afraid that I was going to oversleep. I was up at dawn the next morning and ready to go long before Mr. Hicks came to pick me up.

We left early on a Saturday morning before camp started on Sunday. It was a pretty tense time in the car at first. We had barely met, and we were going to be together for the next 10 hours. No one said anything for miles.

I was self-conscious about my speech difficulty and didn't say much at first. I always had trouble talking to people who didn't know me. I was afraid of what they would think.

Mr. Hicks tried to make Alisa and me feel more comfortable. He was sort of the grandfatherly type, short and stocky with graying hair. He was quiet most of the time, too. We would drive for miles and finally he'd chime in and ask, "How are we making it back there?" directing his question to the back seat where Alisa was. Or he'd turn to me and ask, "Are we doing all right?"

Mom had packed a care package for us to eat on the way. She made homemade chocolate-chip cookies. Mr. Hicks went through those in no time and then he didn't stop for lunch until almost 2 o'clock. I was starving.

As the day wore on, we got a little more relaxed with each other. Once, Mr. Hicks serenaded us with a verse of "You picked a fine time to leave me, Lucille," when a Kenny Rogers song came on the radio. It was all Alisa and I could do to keep from laughing, but it broke the tension and we started talking.

We arrived in Kerrville a little past seven. We stayed in Kerrville that night before going up to camp the next morning. I was excited about spending the night in the motel. The only time I'd stayed in a motel was one summer when we drove to California with Grandma and Granddad Altman.

Mr. Hicks got a room for him and me and an adjoining room for Alisa. Mr. Hicks helped Alisa get settled in her room. She had cerebral palsy, too, though hers was more severe than mine. She could walk with a walker but used a wheelchair most of the time. Mr. Hicks lifted her in and out of her chair when we stopped.

It was my first night away from home, and I was all atwitter. I walked curiously around the motel, gazing wildly at the sites. I couldn't believe I actually had gotten that far.

I didn't think I was tired when I went to bed, but the day's activities must have taken a toll on me. I lay down and the next thing I knew I had dozed off. I guess the excitement of the day had been too much for me because during the night I became violently ill.

I was so anxious about the trip and camp, I made myself sick. My head started swirling, and my stomach was queasy. I tried to get to the bathroom, but I couldn't move; I just lay there. I lost it right there — all over the bed and myself.

Poor Mr. Hicks. He was so vexed by the whole situation he didn't know what to do for me. He helped me into the bathroom, all the while saying, "It's going to be all right. Everything's going to be OK." I think he was trying to convince himself of that more than me, but neither of us was convinced.

Mr. Hicks cleaned up the bed, then helped clean me up. I was so embarrassed. Mr. Hicks helped me change, and we finally got back to sleep, with a little bit of night left.

Things were a lot calmer the next morning. Some of the excitement had dwindled and reality had begun to set in. I thought I might have to go back with Mr. Hicks if I was still as sick as I was the night before. But my stomach had settled and my strength was starting to come back when we got ready to leave.

The camp site was on the outskirts of town, nestled in a clump of tall, slender Pine trees. I had never seen so many trees before, having spent all my life in the flatland area of the Panhandle. It was like being in a different country. By the time we got to the camp, I had forgotten all about being sick.

I expected a great fanfare when we arrived: lots of people milling around, kids laughing and running all over the place. But there was none of that. We were the only ones there. There was a handful of people bustling around setting up tables in the room where we went to register.

Two counselors came and greeted Alisa and me. They said we were just early and that other campers would be arriving soon. The counselors helped us register and took us to our cabins.

Mr. Hicks stayed with me until I got settled. He hung around camp most of the day and said he would check on me before he left in case I had a relapse. I wasn't about to go back with him no matter how sick I was. I had worked too hard to get there; I wasn't going back now.

The cabins were long, barracks-style buildings with concrete floors. It was pretty much what I expected at camp, but the floors were cold and hard, especially when I fell on them. I took several tumbles on the hard floors, and it was quite a jolt.

The inside had three large rooms, with a row of bunks down each side. A couple of the bunks were double-deck. I could never figure out how they expected a disabled person to climb up on the upper bunks, but some did. I was the first one there, so I got first pick. I chose a single-deck bed exactly half way down the row of the beds, so I could be in the center of all the activities.

It was a little tense again before the other campers started arriving. The counselors didn't know what to say, and I was feeling self-conscious again. I couldn't open up and talk with people when I met them. I never could, and I missed out on a lot by not talking and not being more aggressive in starting relationships.

My tribe counselors were Bert Randall and Mike Johnson. They tried to fill the time until the other campers began arriving. A miniature golf course sat back behind our cabin. Bert tried to teach me how to play. I never got the ball in the hole, but I came close a couple of times.

As the day wore on, other campers slowly drifted in. They came with all kinds of disabilities. Some had only slight impairments; others were on crutches and in wheelchairs. Some were deaf, and some had lost an arm or a leg. One boy who became my closest friend at camp was paralyzed from the waist down.

That night after everyone got settled, the camp site was converted into a carnival. The lawn between the bunkhouses became an amusement park. There were game booths, rides and best of all — food! I finally saw the fanfare I had expected since I arrived.

Campers scurried across the lawn on walkers and in wheelchairs, moving from one booth to the next. No longer did the disabilities that had stifled us most of our lives limit our activities. We were regular kids there, doing all the things kids do at camp.

There was an excitement as most of us, for the first time, rivaled in sport and game. It didn't matter if you couldn't do it exactly right; you still won.

I took my turn in the games and won a stuffed animal for tossing a hoop at a pop bottle. I missed the bottle completely, but I won a prize anyway. I was feeling great about myself and about being there.

I passed another booth where they were having a whistling contest and decided to try it. I went up and plunked down my token. I puckered up and started blowing with everything I had.

Nothing happened. I tried again. I took a deep breath and started blowing. Still, no sound came out.

"That's all right," one of the counselors said.

"Try it again," another said.

I tried and tried but could make no sound. Finally, I gave up and as I walked away, I heard one counselor laugh and say to the other, "That one was a spitter."

He didn't say it maliciously. I was trying so hard to force out a sound that spit came out instead. Still, I was angry.

I didn't play any other games the rest of the evening. I just watched. I started getting a little homesick, too. I felt better when the carnival was over and I got back to the cabin. I was exhausted and fell asleep almost as soon as the lights went off.

The days following were planned for us almost from the minute we got up in the morning. Each tribe had activities throughout the day. My tribe started with crafts, followed by recreational sports and swimming in the morning. Then after lunch, we went back out for hiking and nature studies.

For the first time, I didn't have to sit on the sidelines and watch everyone else. I participated. I felt like I really fit in. At school, I was an outsider to many activities because I couldn't do the things the other kids did. But there, I could do everything. We all did.

Lessons in Life

I came to some important realizations on my excursion away from my parents. I realized I had a lot to be thankful for and I needed to make the most of what God had given me. The reason my parents agreed to let me go to camp was that I told them I could take care of myself. But I was still depending on others to do everything for me. Except now, instead of Mom and Dad, I depended on Bert and Mike — and even other campers — to help me.

Most campers needed some help at mealtime, serving their food or cutting it up. The counselors made sure everyone who needed help got it, but I was selfish. I wanted them to do it all for me and when they couldn't do it all, because they had to help the others, I turned to someone else at the table.

Scotty was one of my cabin mates. We became friends during the two weeks we were at camp. Scotty never asked for help. He had no trouble getting his food, so I started relying on him for help.

He cut up my food; he poured the milk on my cereal; he even fed me some of my meals. Everything seemed easy for Scotty.

Scotty only had one arm.

He had lived his whole life with just one arm. I had two good arms, and I was asking him for help. Finally, he said something that woke me up to how fortunate I really was.

We were eating breakfast, and I had finished a bowl of cereal. I was still hungry, so I asked Scotty to get me another bowl.

He turned to me and said, "Why don't you do it yourself?"

"I can't," I said.

"You can't?" he asked in disgust. "I don't think you realize how lucky you are to have two good arms. Stop feeling sorry for yourself and learn to do things for yourself."

He was right. Mom and Dad had been telling me that for a long time, but I wouldn't listen.

"Be glad for what you have and use all that you do have, not what you don't have," Scotty said after a few minutes had passed.

My attitude changed after I talked to Scotty. I started looking around and realized he was right. God had a purpose in making me the way he did. I didn't understand it, but I knew I had a special calling on my life. I wasn't shortchanged from what I didn't have in life. What God takes away physically, he replaces in greater measure.

I gained a greater understanding of what it meant to be disabled after that. I spent the next few days at camp watching the other campers. They were all unique. They each had something special to offer. There was a bond that formed between us as we learned to relate with one another.

There was little time to get bored. Counselors hustled us from one activity to the next. I went swimming every day. I couldn't swim a lick at first; I just sat at the edge of the pool and dangled my feet in the cool water.

Bert urged me to come in the water. "I'll help you," he kept telling me. He gave me a life preserver when I went in the water. I was afraid to go in any farther. I always stayed in the shallow wading area when I went swimming at home, but Bert coaxed me in.

He held me from underneath and cradled me on my back. "Kick your feet now," he instructed. "Wave your arms."

By the time camp was over, I could float. I had to have someone support me to get started, but I could float! I got so excited the first time I almost sank.

"I knew you could do it!" Bert exclaimed. "You can do anything if you want it bad enough."

I discovered I could do a lot of things I never thought possible because of my disability. In crafts, I made a wall ornament out of a piece of tree bark, sand dollars and some pine cones. It took me nearly a week to finish it. I had to glue all the pieces together, then glue it on the bark. Some of the pieces fell off, and I had to paste them on again.

I was so proud of what I had made. I took it home, and Mom hung it up in my room.

At night, all the tribes came together for activities. The camp directors tried to spark some romance between the girls and boys' units by pairing us at a dance.

It was the Saturday after we'd been there a week. All the boys put on clean shirts; the girls wore dresses, and the gymnasium was decorated with paper streamers.

I was reluctant to get out on the dance floor. I wanted to try it, but I couldn't get the nerve to go over and ask anyone to dance. I stood by the wall by myself. It was hysterical to watch. Everybody twitching and shaking! It was hard not to laugh.

About half an hour into the evening, I decided to make my move. I saw a girl on the other side of the room. She was standing alone, too. I walked slowly across the dance floor. What would I say, I thought to myself. Finally, I walked over to her, my heart thumping fiercely as I approached.

". . . Would you dance with me?" I asked quivering. Speaking was frustrating enough, but it was even more difficult to get those words out.

A smile came on her face.

"Yes," she said.

We stepped to the edge of the dance floor and began dancing. It was a fast song; they were all fast songs that night. I never had danced before. I don't think she had either, because neither of us knew what to do. Do I hold her hand? How close do we stand?

I decided not to take her hand. If I held onto her, I might fall and her with me. We stood about a foot apart and swayed back and forth to the music. The hardwood gym floor vibrated beneath us as the beat shook the building. I found a pattern and stuck to it, moving left to right, front to back. I felt silly but was starting to enjoy it when the music stopped. She looked like she enjoyed it too, so I asked her for another dance.

We danced a couple of dances, then I had to sit down. I danced with two other girls that night. I knew I probably would never get the chance to take a regular girl to a dance or go to school dances back home, so I cherished the memories of that night.

During the last few days of camp, the homesickness I started having earlier in the week worsened. I missed home and Mom and Dad. I even missed Karen. Time dragged. It seemed as if I'd been there a month. The longest I'd ever been away from home was overnight, and that was just to sleep over at a friend's house.

I had dreamed of this for such a long time. I never thought I would be homesick. Everybody else was having a good time. I'd see Alisa across the lawn, laughing and singing with the other girls. She looked like she was having the time of her life. I just wanted to go home. It got to the point where I didn't want to do anything. I moped around the cabin all day. Mike and Bert worried about me.

Bert tried to cheer me up by getting me involved in the games. "We're going to play miniature golf. Come play with us," Bert said in a desperate attempt to get me to snap out of it.

I was determined not to play. I just sat under the tall trees by myself. Bert tried to force me to play, taking my arm and leading me over to the golf course.

"It'll help you to forget about missing your folks if you come out and play with us," he said.

I shirked him off. "I said I don't want to play!" I said pulling away from him. He finally just gave up and left me alone. It got so bad at the end that I made myself sick again. They took me to the infirmary the day before camp ended. I was tired and sick and wanted to go home.

We had camp olympics that day before everybody went home. Parents were invited to come down for the competitions and an awards' ceremony that evening. Mom and Dad didn't make it. It was too far for them to come. Alisa's parents came, and then I rode back to Pampa with them.

I left the infirmary in time for the awards' presentation. It was a majestic ceremony held in an outdoor arena. Each olympic winner received medallions. The medals symbolized hard work and determination. It also was a great achievement.

Each tribe presented special achievement awards. Everybody was recognized for something. I got an award for "Most Improved Camper." I didn't feel as if I had done anything to be rewarded. But for many of the kids there, it was the first time they had won at anything. Their faces glowed as they went to receive their awards. It was a night they will never forget.

We left early the next morning to return to Pampa. I was relieved to get home. I grew a lot in the two weeks I was away from my parents. In the weeks following camp, I began to do more for myself.

And when school started in the fall, I was more determined to try harder there, too. I still relied on others for help once in a while, but I saw that I could do more for myself. I began to use what God had given me. I never realized what I had until I saw what many others didn't have. I was more determined to take what I had in life and use it for the best.

Friends

Some of my best friends in life were the ones I made in elementary school. Kids were more accepting at that age. They knew I was different, but it didn't matter. They accepted me and treated me like any other kid.

Bill Luedecke was my best friend growing up. I had known Bill forever it seemed. Bill's mom shared a hospital room with my mom when his brother and my sister were born. They were born just hours apart. Then, when I was 3, Bill's family moved into a house across the street.

We became best friends. We did everything together, but it didn't start out that way. Bill was a ruffian as a boy, a brawler. He was afraid of nothing and no one. One day, Bill and some of the neighborhood kids were out in the yard when I went out to play. Bill was the new kid on the street and hadn't been around me much.

When I asked him if I could play, he shoved me down. "You can't play with us. Go on home," he said. Crushed, I ran home crying.

Dad was watching from the window, as he often did when I went outdoors, and saw Bill push me. Not willing that anyone should pick on his little boy, Dad marched over and told Bill's mother that her son was picking on me. From that day on, Bill and I were closer than brothers. In fact, he stuck up for me whenever other kids picked on me.

Over the years, Bill was the one true friend who always stood by me. He accepted me despite my limitations. He always thought of me when it was time to do something, while others often left me out of their activities. Nothing stood in our way as we powered around the neighborhood on our bicycles.

My parents bought me a three-wheel bicycle. At first, Dad wouldn't let me take it off the block. Bill and I rode up and down the street time after time. Bill refused to leave me when I had to stop at the corner and all the other kids kept going. Bill stuck by me.

Finally, Dad let me take it around the block. Then it was two blocks. Then three, until one day we just kept going. Soon, we were riding all over town, and nothing could stop us.

We told Bill's mom everywhere we went because she didn't care what we did as long as we told her where we were going, while my mom would have had a fit if she'd known half the places we went on our bikes. So, we thought it best not to tell her most of the places we went.

It was also at that stage in my life when I began to notice the difference between boys and girls. I had my first school-boy crush in the fourth grade. Kambra Winningham. She was the most popular girl in the class and the brightest, and I set my sights on making her my girlfriend. So, in the fourth grade, I asked Kambra to go with me. That was the thing to do in the fourth grade to be "going together."

When I got Kambra on the phone, my tongue got tied in knots, and I didn't know what to say.

"Kambra, This is Chris . . . Ely," I said finally, trying to get the words out without stuttering and stammering.

"Hi, Chris," she said sounding surprised to hear from me.

"Uh, I was wondering . . . did you bring your math book home?" I asked trying desperately to come up with an excuse for calling.

"No, we didn't have any homework in math." she said sounding puzzled.

"Oh, that's right. Well, uh, are you . . . are you going with anybody?" I asked knowing perfectly well that she didn't have a beau.

"What?"

"Are you going with anyone?"

"You mean do I have a boyfriend?"

"Yes."

"No, I'm not going with anyone right now."

By now, I'm sure she knew where I was going with this, so I figured it was time to quit stalling and just come out and ask her.

"Kambra, will you go with me?"

There was a long pause, then she said softly, "I'm sorry, Chris, I can't go with you."

My heart sank.

"I think you're a very nice boy, and you're very special," she continued, "but I can't go with you. I'm sorry."

She tried to let me down easy, and she was very nice about the whole thing.

"It's all right," I said fighting back tears and a big lump in my throat. "I understand." I really did understand why she had to say no, and I didn't have any hard feelings against her.

"I'll see you at school tomorrow, OK?" she asked.

"OK. Bye," I said wanting to end the humiliation as quickly as possible.

I hung up the phone heartbroken. She had said no. I did understand, though. She hadn't turned me down because I had cerebral palsy. She would have had to turn me down no matter who I was because we were just so different.

Kambra wouldn't have hurt me for anything in the world. She walked up to me in the hall the next day.

"I hope you're not angry at me," she said.

"No," I said even though I was disappointed. "We can still be friends, can't we?"

"Yes, of course. I've always thought of you as one of my best friends."

Kambra became one of my closest friends later on in high school and stayed in contact long after we left school.

Soon after that, though, I set my sights on another girl. And this time, she said yes. Joni Hagerman. We had been in class together since the second grade, and we had developed a special friendship through the years. Joni had a bright smile and a wonderful sense of humor. She loved to laugh, even at my feeble attempts to be funny. She always laughed.

She wasn't uncomfortable around me the way others were. I often was self-conscious about my handicap when I was around others. I pulled away and wouldn't let people get close. I was afraid they would reject me because I was different.

It was different with Joni. I could be myself. It didn't matter that I couldn't keep up when we walked on the playground together. We just enjoyed spending time together.

We hardly saw each other outside of school, but I wrote her notes on the typewriter nearly every night. She wrote notes, too, and then we passed them in class the next day. If we got caught, we were sure to have them picked up and read to the entire class. Still, everyone did it and risked getting caught.

One night, I got up the courage to call Joni. I was so nervous as my hands fidgeted to dial the phone. I hoped Joni would answer so I wouldn't have to talk to her mom or worse, her dad.

Once I got her on the phone, though, I was at a loss for words.

"Joni? This is Chris," I said.

"Chris, hi!" she said sounding surprised to her from me.

"What are you doing tonight?"

"We just got through with dinner."

"Oh."

There was a long break of silence on the phone.

Then she asked, "What are you doing?"

"Nothing. I went to visit my grandmother."

"Oh, that's nice."

Pause.

"Uh, have you finished your homework?" I asked for a lack of anything else to say.

"Yes, I finished it at school," she said.

"Me too."

Pause.

"Well, I guess I'll see you tomorrow."

"OK."

"OK . . . Well, bye."

"See ya."

The call lasted all of five minutes. We didn't really say anything, but it was just the fact that we had talked to each other that mattered. We really enjoyed our friendship. But then one of the girls in our class started teasing us about going together. "Chris and Joni — love birds," she would say mockingly. Kids can be so cruel. Finally, it got the better of us, and Joni and I broke up. I was crushed because I cherished our friendship.

As I got older, it was harder for me to make friends like the ones I had in elementary school. Because of my speech problem, I pulled back and wouldn't talk to people unless they spoke to me first. I wouldn't let people get close to me. I was afraid of what they would think, afraid they wouldn't accept me. That's what made the memories of the times I spent with my friends in grade school so special.

The move to junior high school was a difficult one, but one I faced head-on. The challenges of familiarity were enough for me without trying to cope with new ones. I was starting a new school, with new people and new challenges.

I stopped going to the rehabilitation center when I got to junior high. Mom and Dad were afraid I would miss too much school and lag behind the other students if I kept going. The therapists told them there was hardly anything else they could do for me in a medical sense. My speech was as clear as it was ever going to get, and any further improvement was up to what I wanted to do for myself.

It was only the year before that the physical therapist took me out of my braces. It wasn't that my walking had improved so much that I didn't need them anymore, but the muscles in my legs had grown too strong for the braces, and the shoes weren't doing the job they were meant to.

The only thing they hadn't tried was surgery. The doctors said I might have a chance to improve my walking if they reset the bones in my legs. They wanted to break my legs and rejoin the bones, hoping it would straighten my walking. Dad wouldn't hear of this. He probably would have agreed if it would help me, but there was no guarantee my walking would get any better.

I was relieved Dad wouldn't allow the surgery. Not to mention being quite painful, I didn't want to think about learning how to walk all over again. Not now when I was just starting junior high.

I was ecstatic the day at the center when Mr. Balke told me I no longer had to wear the braces, which had so conspicuously set me apart from other children. I had dreamed of the day I could wear sneakers to school. I was so excited. I nagged Mom until she took me down to the store and we bought my first pair of tennis shoes.

I could hardly wait to get home so I could show off my new shoes to Karen and all the neighborhood kids. The shoes were softer on my feet than the heavy orthopedic oxfords. I was so proud of my new shoes. That evening, I strolled down the sidewalk in my new sneakers. A neighbor was working in her yard when I passed.

Suddenly, she stopped and looked up at me. "Chris, you're not making any noise!" she exclaimed.

The neighbor noticed I wasn't making the racket I usually made when I passed her house. With my soft-soled shoes, I didn't make the loud clatter when I clomped down the sidewalk. The neighbor shared my elation over my shoes.

My new shoes did a lot to feed my weak ego, especially as I started junior high the next year. I didn't stand out as I did in my twisters, but there was still enough other differences to make me not fit in. Junior high was a whole new experience.

Things I took for granted before I had to work at in junior high. There was talk about putting me in special education classes. Classes were a little harder in junior high and the pace a little faster, and some of the teachers wondered if I would be able to keep up.

Dad was dead set against the idea of special classes. I had made it in regular classes before; I could do it now, he insisted.

Dad knew I would need some special training, but he didn't want me in special education. He conceded to let them continue giving me speech therapy at school, and he agreed that I shouldn't take gym or music. I had gone to music and gym before, but now they didn't think I could keep up with the other students. The problem was no one knew what to do with me during those two hours every day, so they stuck me in a special ed class.

I was separated from the rest of the class. They put me at a little desk in the corner, got me a typewriter and let me do my homework. But I didn't belong there. I didn't want to be there. The other students in the class had learning disabilities. I didn't. But there was nowhere else for me to go. So I was stuck there — to be baby-sat.

I watched the other students. I knew I was different from the others. They were working on basic addition and subtraction, and I was doing regular math. It wasn't that I thought I was better than they were, but their problems were different from mine.

I was bored in the class. I would sit in front of the typewriter and try to study, but all I could think about was the kids in the regular classes. I wondered what they were doing in music. I wanted to do what they were doing. I wanted to be with them, but instead I was in a class where the teacher was a baby sitter.

Friday was game day. If everyone finished all their work, we got to play games while just down the hall I could hear the other students still hard at work. I would have much rather been down there still working than where I was just playing.

There were other hurdles to cross starting a new school. The school was larger than my old school. There were nearly twice as many students, and with that many people milling, pushing and jostling their way through the halls, Mom and Dad worried I'd get trampled in the crowd.

Instead of staying in one classroom for every subject, now I had to make my way to a different classroom and a different teacher.

Dad was an art teacher at the school — which proved to have good and bad sides in itself — so he tried to get my classes moved closer together. He also asked the teachers to let me leave class five minutes early so I could move freely through the empty halls.

Even with a five-minute head start, I often arrived at class late and out of breath. It was a race against the clock. If I could make it within striking distance of my next class, I had a chance. I knew that at any second the bell would sound, releasing the savages from their cages. It was every man for himself then. I plowed my way through the unmindful crowd to keep from going down for the count, dodging bodies and darting through the door before the second bell rang. That was the end of round one.

I used a wheelchair to go to the cafeteria and for longer trips. I hated being pushed in a wheelchair. It was faster than walking, and it was certainly easier, but I had to ask someone to take me where I wanted to go and I wanted to do it, as much as I could, on my own.

My classmates took turns pushing the wheelchair. My grade-school pal Derrick took his turn pushing me and turned the hallway into a speedway. We raced down the hall coming back from lunch. I was afraid we were going to hit somebody and hurt them.

We'd take off down the hall, weaving in and out of traffic. I just closed my eyes and prayed we didn't hit anyone. People scrambled to clear the way for us. We nicked a few heels with the foot rest a time or two, but no one was seriously maimed. We got through the crowd in record time. We usually made it to class just in the nick of time before the bell rang. That was the end of round two.

Making the Grade

It was in the first year in junior high that I realized I could do more with the potential God had given me. Always before, I had looked at school as a place to go and be with my friends, and I didn't take school as seriously as I ought.

When I got to junior high, that all began to change. With Dad there, I had to be on my best behavior. I could no longer get by with doing the things I had done in grade school. Dad knew everything I did. When I got in trouble in class, the teacher wouldn't send me to the principal's office. She marched down to Dad's room and told him what I had done.

Mom and Dad never put any unrealistic expectations on Karen or me to get good grades. All they asked was that we did our best. But I made up my mind that I was going to work hard and get good grades that year. Having Dad at the same school was all the more reason to do well. The teachers expected me to get good grades because I was Charles Ely's boy.

It was nearing the end of the first quarter of the semester, six-weeks tests time. I had just gotten by all six weeks, and now it was time to get serious. Mom helped me study every night after dinner. She'd give out the questions, and I'd retort the answers. We continued this routine each night before the tests.

The hard work paid off when I got my math test back and got my first 'A.' I realized then that I could be a good student if I worked at it. I felt as if I had really accomplished something — like I had really succeeded — and Mom and Dad were elated. I had a good feeling knowing I had done my best and got something for my effort.

I knew I would never be a great athlete or set any records in sports, but I could succeed academically. Everyone is given different abilities, and it's up to each person to use what God has given him. I never was content to just get by anymore.

I worked harder that year than I ever had before. I hit the books as soon as I got home from school each day, and it took me all evening sometimes to finish my homework. But I couldn't rest until I got it done. It wasn't easy. But, anything that is worthwhile never is. I worked hard all year and was on the B-honor roll every six weeks.

My weak point was reading. I hated reading. It was a bad trait for someone who would grow up and one day be a newspaperman and depend on reading for his livelihood, but I just didn't like to read.

I put off reading assignments as long as I could, and many times just skimmed over the material before class. There was one teacher who invariably would give a pop quiz over the reading. He loved to give pop tests, and he always seemed to give them on the occasions when I hadn't read. Even when I read the assignment, I panicked when he gave a surprise test.

I wanted so desperately to do well that I was even willing to cheat for good grades, letting my eyes wander in search of the right answers. Russ Rabel sat across the aisle from me in history class. He was the smartest boy in the class. I thought if I could peak at his paper, I could get a couple of the questions right.

I'd drop my pencil on the floor, then when I bent over to pick it up, I'd glance at his paper. I knew it was wrong, but the desire to make good grades was stronger than any moral values that had been so sternly drilled into me.

Trouble was, I always felt guilty afterward. Tormented by my conscience, I swore I'd never cheat again. But the next day, I found myself doing the same thing.

Russ knew I looked at his paper. One day, he came right out and told me to stop looking at his paper.

"It's not going to do you any good anyway," he said. "I don't read it either."

I was so embarrassed that he saw me copying that I vowed never to do it again. I didn't want him to think of me as a cheat. I knew it was wrong to look, and I made myself keep my eyes on my own paper, even if the result was a bad grade.

It turned out that the teacher didn't grade the tests most of the time. He just gave them so we would read. It was a valuable lesson any way. I had to rely on my efforts to get me through and whatever happened I had to learn to accept the consequences.

My greatest fear came true in the seventh grade: I got my dad for a teacher. I had dreaded this moment ever since I started to school there. It was a small school, and there was only one or two teachers for each subject.

Dad was the only art teacher for all of the seventh grade. I didn't have to take art that year, but I think Dad would have been a little disappointed if I hadn't taken his class.

Karen took his class when she went to school there, and he kind of expected me to take it, too. Besides, I was curious to see what kind of teacher he was. I never thought of him the way I thought about a teacher, so this was going to be a new experience — for both of us.

It was hard enough having him at the same school. I couldn't walk down the halls without seeing him. He knew every move I made.

Now, I was going to be in his class. There ought to be a rule to keep parents from having their own children in class. I was terrified on the first day of school. What do I call him? Do I address him as Mr. Ely or Dad? What if I forgot and called him Dad by mistake?

I walked in and sat down at a table at the back of the room. I tried to look inconspicuous. It was a large class, so I just tried to blend in.

It was surprisingly fun the first day. Dad got up and talked about the projects we'd be working on during the semester. It was mainly drawing and painting the first semester. Then, the second half, we'd be doing some work with clay and pottery. He actually made it sound fun.

Then, when I thought he couldn't surprise me anymore than he already had, he did something that completely shocked me. He told a joke during class. I couldn't believe it.

Was this really my dad? My dad wasn't funny. Everyone in class thought he was great. Maybe I had misjudged my dad. Maybe this wasn't going to be as bad as I had imagined.

It must have been as awkward for him as it was for me. I raised my hand to ask a question one day, and he said, "Yes, you in the back, did you have a question?" Everyone in class burst out laughing. Everyone knew I was Mr. Ely's son. That's how they referred to me. "You're Mr. Ely's son," they'd say.

Dad tried to be impartial and showed me no favors. He treated me like any other student in the class. Once, when he thought I was talking too much, he made me write "I will not talk" 25 times on a piece of paper. I couldn't believe it. My own father.

Sometimes, he was too impartial when it came to me. I never professed to be any good at drawing or at art in general. In fact, it was difficult for me to do many of the things we did in the class because of my poorly coordinated hands. Some tasks, like cutting and gluing, were impossible. Dad had to help me. Still, I did all of the projects and I tried.

So, I couldn't believe it when I got my first report card and saw he had given me a 'B' and kept me off the honor roll! My homeroom teacher, Mr. Wyatt, came down to Dad's room one morning before school and said, "Mr. Ely, I think you better have a look at your son's report card."

I was scared. I thought I had really done something wrong when Mr. Wyatt brought in my report card. Dad looked at the report card; then, he looked over at me.

"Well, what do you have to say about that?" Mr. Wyatt asked.

"I don't know," Dad said looking at me again.

By that time, I was really getting worried. I thought I had done pretty well in all my classes. What had I done wrong?

"Maybe we should show your son what you've done to him," Mr. Wyatt said.

I picked up the paper and begin to study it carefully. It had all 'A's on it. All except one. A 'B' in art. I missed making the A-honor roll by two points.

"How could you do that to your own son?" Mr. Wyatt asked.

He razzed Dad about keeping me off the honor roll all semester. Mr. Wyatt wouldn't let him forget it. Mom gave him a hard time about it, too. Dad insisted that he gave me what he thought I deserved, and I didn't want him to give me something I hadn't earned.

So, the next six weeks, I worked even harder so I would make all 'A's. And Dad saw my effort. He gave me two more points to get a 90 in the class. He didn't give it to me. I worked for it, and Dad agreed that I had earned it.

Father and Son

M om went back to work that year after 15 years at home.
She had worked at the electric company for 10 years
before Karen and I were born.

When Karen was born, she quit to stay home and take
care of her. After I was born, she couldn't work. All of her
time was consumed taking care of me, taking me to Amarillo for therapy every week and helping me with school.

As I got older, I stopped going to the center, and Karen
was out of the house more. Mom had more spare time on
her hands. I'm not sure if Mom was really looking to go
back to work. But when they called and asked her if she
wanted to come back to work, Mom decided to do it.

She gave 15 years of undying care to her family. Now, it
was time she did something for herself. We all had to make
adjustments. Dad had to help out around the house. Some
days, he would have dinner started when Mom got home.
Dad didn't use cookbooks. He just sort of made up his
own recipe as he went along, and some of the strange con-
coctions he came up with were hardly edible.

He mixed the strangest things together — corn in the mashed potatoes, beans with eggs. "It all goes to the same place in the end," he said.

It was strange coming home from school and not finding Mom there. Mom and I shared a special bond. We spent a lot of time together, when it was just her and me. She spent countless hours doing so much for me and helping me. She gave so much love to her family.

It was different being home alone with Dad. Karen worked after school, and Mom didn't get off until after 5. That left about an hour that Dad and I were there by ourselves.

I had a different kind of relationship with my dad than I had with Mom. Dad showed his affection in a different way. He didn't pacify me the way Mom did. Dad was a strong man but very private.

Dad kept to himself most of the time. He had a lot of health problems and didn't like to go out much. He preferred a quiet night at home to going out. Mom said he would have stayed home from his own wedding if he had the choice. I could never understand his wanting to stay home all the time, and he thought if he didn't go out, Mom and us kids shouldn't go anywhere either. He was happy if we never went anywhere.

When Mom tried to get him to go to a restaurant, Dad practically refused.

"Why don't you go and bring me something back," he would say.

We went without him some, but Mom didn't feel right leaving him home alone. It created a strain between them, so most of the time we stayed home.

It was worse when Mom started working, and I stayed home with Dad, especially with summer coming on. Mom and I could always find things to do together. It wasn't like that with Dad. We couldn't go out and toss the football around in the yard. We couldn't throw the baseball back and forth to each other. We couldn't do many of the things fathers and sons do together.

Dad did take me fishing. We would drive down to the lake for a day of trout fishing. But there was always a strife that existed between my father and me that distanced us and kept us from drawing closer.

I don't know if, subconsciously, I blamed him for my infirmity. Or maybe I felt inadequate, like I couldn't be the kind of son he wanted. Whatever it was, it drove a wedge between us.

It was never a matter of love. I loved my father deeply, and I know he loved me. He provided for me in ways I knew nothing about until years later. He supported everything I strived to do. And even when I failed, Dad was there to pick me up and tell me to keep going.

Yet, there was still that division that kept us from bonding as father and son. Maybe it was just a rebellious period that many teen-agers go through where they must test authority to prove their own security.

I hurt my dad deeply. It wasn't something that he had done. I had to deal with my insecurity about my disability, and he became the target. Over time, I was able to expel the feelings of doubt, and I realized how much his love meant to me.

It took time for the wounds to heal. I regret it took so long for me to see how strong his love was. We had a chance to share time together when it was just him and me in the house, and I let it slip away.

That time was lost forever. I can never take back the things I did. Fortunately, time and love brought us closer together. I was never able to talk to Dad the way I talked to my mom, but Dad and I came to have a special relationship, too.

Although it was difficult for both of us to reveal our feelings, I cherished what we had together and what our love was able to endure.

The Search for Acceptance

From the time I started school, there had been no other students with disabilities in school when I was. It was lonely as I tried to find acceptance among my classmates. Although they were gracious and wanted to help, they didn't welcome me into their groups with outstretched arms. I often found myself standing alone on the playground at lunch.

I was an outsider, looking for someone who would give me a chance for who I was. I felt like I was the only one who had ever tried to survive in a world of able-bodied people. Of course, I wasn't the only one nor was I the first one to ever go to regular school.

There were those who came before me, but schools were only just beginning to realize the potential of disabled students to lead normal lives.

It hadn't been too many years before that the disabled didn't have the opportunity to go to school. They were kept at home and weren't allowed to try. In the early part of this century, when someone was born with a crippling disease, they were hidden away in a room somewhere, often out of sight.

It was considered a part of nature, and people didn't talk about it outside the family. Families took care of their own. People didn't have the resources to take care of the disabled, so they put them in a back room somewhere, where they had to be content to stay all their lives.

It wasn't meant to be cruel. It's just the way it was. People didn't realize that disabled people could lead normal, productive lives. Gradually, times began to change, and people came to see that the disabled could be productive.

I realized how fortunate I was to be getting an education. I was one of the lucky ones. I had been around many disabled kids at the center, but I had never gone to school with one. Then, in my last year in junior high, for the first time, I encountered one of my own: another CP student.

Timmy looked like any other student. It was the first day back after the long summer vacation, and he stumbled into my last-period class and sat down on the front row.

He arrived late, carrying a briefcase stuffed full of wrinkled papers; his hair was ruffled, he looked tired and confused. It looked like the first day of school had been too much for him.

He looked like a dazed sixth-grader who had gotten lost and stumbled into our class by mistake. Timmy was small for his age. Everyone else in the room towered over him by a head. He didn't look like an eighth-grader, nor did he look like he was supposed to be in that class.

I didn't realize he was disabled at first. He had a milder form of cerebral palsy than mine. He had a slight limp, but it was hardly noticeable as he walked into the room.

As class got under way, it became clear that he was in the right place after all, and I soon realized that he had cerebral palsy.

His speech was slurred to a degree that made it a little hard to understand when he answered the roll, and he seemed to have difficulty writing.

He noticed me right away. He kept looking over his shoulder at me during class. He apparently was just as curious about me as I was about him.

"Finally, someone I can relate to," I thought to myself. "Someone who's going through the same thing I am."

After class, he came over and talked to me. Trouble was I couldn't understand him, and he couldn't understand me. Suddenly, I realized how others must have felt trying to talk to me.

This time, I was the one not understanding. I'd ask Timmy to repeat things; then I still didn't understand all he was saying. I shook my head in agreement as if I had understood.

I hated it when people did that to me. I'd try to say something or ask them a question, and they'd have no idea what I had said. But they would just nod their heads because they were too embarrassed or too afraid to ask me to repeat it.

It was harder to communicate with Timmy than I had imagined. We both stumbled over words and struggled to understand each other. But after we talked awhile, he was easy to understand. I had to learn to listen, which is what others had to do with me.

Timmy hadn't lived the sheltered life I had. His life was exciting compared to mine. His parents were missionaries to Mexico when he was a boy. His family moved around a

lot, and he saw a different culture as they traveled throughout Central America. Timmy learned the language and
could speak Spanish fluently. In fact, Spanish was easier
for him than English.

Timmy went to a private, Christian school for much of
his early schooling. He started eighth grade in the public
school system. What a cultural shock it must have been
coming into the public schools. He had gone to private
school most of his life, where there was more acceptance.
There were a lot of adjustments, and over the school year
we learned to help each other.

It helped having a friend who faced the same toils and
trials. I no longer felt as if I was all alone. I felt a closeness
with Timmy. I was no longer singled out in class because I
was different and had to use different methods for com-
pleting assignments.

I had only one class with Timmy that semester. It was a
life-science class. We learned about the different kinds of
little creeping critters. We studied crustaceans and all the
life forms. We had to dissect insects — and a frog. It was
the only class I'd been in where we were graded for playing
with bugs.

In one experiment, we cut an inch worm in half and
watched it every day until it regenerated itself by growing
back its lost parts. It was a simple experiment that didn't
require a lot of effort. But for Timmy and me, the simplest
experiments were difficult when you have trouble managing a dissecting knife.

One day, the teacher paired the class in teams of two for
the experiment. She left out Timmy and me when she divided the class. She directed each team to a lab table and
began explaining the procedure. Meanwhile, Timmy and I

were left sitting at our desks. I couldn't figure out why we weren't being included in the experiment. I was angry because I thought she was leaving us out.

She finished explaining the experiment to the rest of the class, then she turned to us. "Chris and Timmy, would you come up here please," she said as she returned to her tall lab desk.

I still didn't know what was going on. Timmy and I looked at each other with confusion. We thought we had done something wrong. I didn't think I had done anything. Why had she singled us out? We nervously made our way to the front.

Finally, the teacher cleared up the mystery. "Would you two like to work together on this experiment?" she asked. "I know it's kind of hard for you to do some of the experiments, but I think you can do this one."

I looked at Timmy. He looked pleased with the idea, and I was definitely intrigued by it. Always before when we had lab, we had to watch while someone else did the actual operation.

"All right," we said in unison.

"You two will make a good team, and you can work and help each other," she said.

Timmy and I joined the rest of the class at the lab tables, and the teacher gave each set of partners a worm. It created a stir among some girls in the class who became squeamish when she put one of the squiggly little creatures on the dissection pan.

It was an easy procedure. All we had to do was to take the knife and slice the worm in two. Timmy pinned down the worm on the pan, then I made the cut. Then, we placed a cover over the pan to protect the worm, and that was it.

There was nothing hard about it, but it meant a lot more to me because I got to participate in the experiment. I didn't have to stand aside and watch while someone else did everything. I actually took part in the experiment.

And it helped having someone in the class who was my peer, an equal in every way. Timmy and I became close friends over the next few months. Our infirmity put us on common ground. We found that we shared many of the same dreams and aspirations, experienced the same heartaches.

"I'm the same as anybody else," he once told me. "I can do the same as any other student, or at least should have the chance to try."

That's all I ever wanted. That's all most disabled people want — the chance to make their dreams come true. All they ask is that they have the same opportunities in life as anybody else.

Speaking Out

∞

Talking was a real frustration to me in school because most teachers were never around me enough to learn my speech pattern. If there was ever a time when I was relieved people couldn't comprehend my parlance, it was when I cut up in class.

I got by with things that otherwise would have gotten me an instant trip to the principal's office, because the teacher didn't understand me. Wisecracks and pearls of sarcasm dripped from my lips during class, only to be dismissed because the teacher didn't know what I had said. I had a quick response if the teacher asked me to repeat.

A friend of mine, Mike Ballard, sat behind me in English class. He always started laughing when I made one of my wisecracks. My classmates who were around me all day understood me better than the teacher who only saw me for an hour once a day. Everyone in class knew exactly what I said and laughed at my cracks, which is the real reason I did it. I wanted them to like me and accept me.

The teacher hardly thought my interruptions were funny. She would give me a piercing look. Thankfully, she never knew what I was whispering about, but she constantly had to tell me to be quiet.

One six weeks I was especially disruptive. Mike and I talked constantly during class, chatting when we should have been paying attention. When report cards came out that quarter, Mike and I received unsatisfactory conduct grades.

I never had been afraid to take a report card home, but that six weeks I didn't want my parents to see my report card. Mom and Dad didn't get too upset over grades, as long as I had done my best, but they were furious if I brought home a bad conduct grade.

All day I had worried about showing them my report card. I had done pretty well that six weeks, but it was the first time I had gotten a "U." I wasn't sure how they'd react, so I prepared for the worse. Finally, I decided to come right out and show it to Dad.

I went straight to Dad's room after school. "Did you get your report card?" was the first thing he asked me.

I thought maybe he wouldn't notice it when I handed him the card. I thought he might be so pleased with my grades that he wouldn't notice my conduct grade. Then, a serious, sullen look came over Dad's face. He had seen it — the big "U" in the right column.

"What's this?" Dad demanded.

"What?" I asked innocently.

"You know what. Why did you get an unsatisfactory in English class?" Dad knew all my teachers of course. He saw them every day, so it was embarrassing for Dad when his own son got in trouble.

"I guess I talked too much." I said. I didn't tell Dad I had been making wisecracks, too.

"Well, do you want your spanking now or when we get home?"

I burst out crying right there. "I'm sorry. I won't talk in class anymore," I said sobbing.

Dad blistered my bottom when we got home. The next day, he had a long talk with my English teacher. He assured her that she would have no more trouble out of me and told her to let him know if I started talking again.

I learned my lesson. I didn't say another word during class the entire semester.

You have to laugh at your shortcomings. It's the only way you can survive sometimes, but I went about it the wrong way, trying to get others to like me by using my speech impediment to gain acceptance. I felt guilty about using my handicap to trick others into liking me.

I knew if I was ever going to achieve anything in life, hard work and determination would carry me a long way toward success. As I prepared to say good-bye to Pampa Middle School, I started looking to the future. It was disheartening to think I'd soon be leaving that place, where I shared so many good times. I had made giant strides there.

As hard as it was starting junior high, it was harder to leave. The Friday before school was out, the entire class gathered in the auditorium for the honors assembly. It was like a graduation ceremony. Students who had excelled during the year were recognized at the assembly with awards for achievements in sports, music and academics.

The top students in the class received special commendations. They were the ones who had the highest grades. I knew I had a ways to go before I reached that point, so it came as a surprise to me when the principal called my name during the assembly.

I was shocked. I hadn't expected to win an award. I knew my grades weren't high enough to make the top cut in the class. I didn't know why I would be getting an award. They honored me as the student who showed the most potential.

Dad came to the assembly and stood at the back of the auditorium. He didn't know about the award, only that he needed to be there. The award came as a surprise to him, too. He was standing in the back of the auditorium and got to see me walk down and receive the award.

I was ecstatic. All my hard work had paid off. I had a great feeling of accomplishment when I left school that day.

As I walked home, I thanked God for what he had allowed me to do. I remembered that verse I learned in Sunday school. In Philippians, it says "I can do all things through Christ who strengthens me." God was my strength. I had to ask for his help daily, and he went with me and provided the way.

I felt privileged to be able to do everything I did. It was truly a gift from God. I soon would be leaving junior high, and I was uncertain what the future held for me. I didn't know if I'd be able to succeed in high school as I had in junior high, but I just trusted the Lord to help me. I knew with his help, I would succeed in everything I did.

Sister's Big Day

As I prepared to leave junior high and looked to high school looming on the horizon, a new day also was dawning on my sister. Karen was nearing her final days in school and soon would be out on her own.

With Karen gone, I stood to get all the attention. I'd have Mom and Dad all to myself. Not that I didn't get plenty of attention already. Growing up, I took up more of Mom and Dad's time. Karen may have felt a little left out with my parents rushing around taking me to the center and doctors' appointments, but she never complained. She unselfishly sacrificed for me.

Karen was looking to her graduation now, a big day in anybody's life. It's the culmination of 12 years of hard work and determination, all for the moment when you step across the stage and receive a diploma.

And Karen was poised to take her place on that stage. She would cross the stage and into a whole new world. It was an exciting time around our house as we celebrated

Karen's joy. My sister's graduation put our whole household in a dither.

I always figured Karen would get married after graduation. Karen was a popular girl and had a lot of friends in school, but it wasn't until her sophomore year that she started to discover the opposite sex. Then, she fell head over heels. Karen took an instant liking to Dean Linder.

Dean was a stocky fellow. He had coal-black hair and a dark complexion. He was a year older than Karen.

Dad was very protective of both me and Karen. We thought he was overly protective. When Karen started seeing Dean, Dad insisted that she wait until she was 16 before she began dating.

Karen, of course, was furious. She thought Dad was a tyrant. It was still a year and a half until her 16th birthday, and to her, that seemed like an eternity.

That didn't keep her from seeing Dean, though. They couldn't go out, so Dean came over to the house every day after school and stayed until nearly supper. Then, after dinner he called her, and they spent another hour on the phone. Nothing could keep them apart.

They dated all through high school and always talked about getting married when Karen finished school. But no one was ready for the conversation Karen sprang on us one spring day at the dinner table.

"How soon before a wedding do you ask the preacher to marry you?" she asked.

Mom nearly dropped her fork. She was so surprised. "Well . . . it's usually a couple of months before," Mom said, trying to contain herself.

"I guess we need to talk to the pastor now, then."

Karen shocked us all with the news. She and Dean planned to get married right after graduation. Mom and

Dad had hoped they would wait awhile after she finished school, at least until June and her 18th birthday, but they couldn't wait.

Dean had finished school the year before and was living in Amarillo, taking classes at the college and working at night. He wanted Karen to join him as soon as she got out of school.

I don't think anyone was prepared for what happened next. Karen informed us they had set the date for May 28. Mom and Dad were completely put back.

They tried to talk her into waiting a little while so they would have time to plan. But Karen and Dean were in love; they couldn't wait until they could be together.

So, it was set. The wedding would take place May 28, two days after Karen's high school graduation. That didn't leave much time.

It turned our household upside down as Mom scurried to put together a wedding in a little less than two months. Karen and Dean said they didn't want a big wedding. They wanted a simple ceremony with just the family and a few friends.

There was still much to do to get ready for the wedding. Invitations had to be mailed out; the church had to be booked and, of course, Karen had to find her dress.

I never fully realized that my sister would be leaving until a couple of weeks before the wedding. Karen and I fought like any normal brother and sister growing up, but deep down I loved her, and I think she cared about me. It was hard to imagine what it would be like when she left.

I told everyone I wouldn't miss her. After all, I had a lot to gain. With her leaving, I stood to inherit a larger bedroom. Karen's room was the corner room. A huge closet stretched across one end of the room. I always said I wanted that room when Karen left.

As the day of the big event got closer, it hit me that she really was leaving. She would no longer be there to boss me around. I wouldn't have anybody to tease. One thing was for sure — our lives would never be the same again.

There was a bustle of activity as graduation day approached. It seemed a shame that Karen's graduation was somewhat overshadowed by plans for the wedding. It was still a big occasion for Karen. It just seemed like she was rushing it, instead of taking time to revel in the moment.

In some ways, Karen was doubly blessed. It's not too many people who find true happiness and know exactly what they want right out of school. She knew exactly what she wanted out of life and followed her heart. I was always a little jealous of her. All our lives, I had watched as she discovered all that she could do with her life, while I fought to keep control of mine.

Mom and Karen were both exhausted by the time her graduation finally arrived. It was a hot, sultry evening as we packed into the high school fieldhouse to watch my sister graduate. It was an emotional night. Everyone was all teary-eyed. Mom had been crying for weeks. She couldn't bear the thought of her only daughter leaving home. Dad was taking it all in stride. And I think Karen was a little nervous that night, too.

I was proud of her as she got her diploma — proud that she was my sister and proud of what she'd achieved. I couldn't help but think, however, of the day that I would walk across that stage. I saw how happy Karen was, and I wanted to have that same happiness, too, someday.

The next day and a half were a blur. Karen and Mom were up at dawn the next morning making last-minute preparations at the church. They planned to have the wedding in the vestibule, just off the main sanctuary. It was a cozy, little room, but large enough to seat about 60.

Dean and Karen insisted that they didn't want a big ceremony, so this was the next best thing. They had magnificent sprays of flowers strategically placed about the room. It was beautiful. It looked like something out of a fairy tale.

I barely had a chance to see Karen the day before the wedding. That evening, everyone met for the rehearsal ceremony. Dad was so nervous. For his part in the ceremony, he had to escort Karen down the aisle. Then, when the preacher asked who gives this woman, Dad was supposed to say, "Her mother and I."

He must have practiced saying it 10 different ways before he decided how to say it. He first tried saying it in a deep, scraggly voice. Then, he said it in his natural voice. It was quite humorous really. After that, the bride and groom said their vows.

I forced back a laugh when they started talking about love and all that until-death-do-you-part stuff. Then, when it was time for the groom to kiss the bride, I had to laugh. I guess I was still too young to understand that mushy love stuff. Mom shot me a silencing glance from across the aisle. She scolded me after the rehearsal and told me I better not try anything during the ceremony.

I don't think anyone got any sleep that night. I know Karen didn't sleep. There was electricity in the air; the excitement was building. I still found it hard to believe that in one more day, Karen would be gone.

Of course, she'd only be an hour's drive away from home. We'd still see her, but it would never be the same again. I felt closer to Karen than I ever had.

I didn't think I got any sleep that night, but I must have dozed off some time because when I woke up it was morning. I felt the way you do on Christmas morning, with that feeling of excitement and suspense knotted up in the pit of my stomach. It was a joyous feeling. I was genuinely happy for my sister.

Karen was already hustling around the house. It was like a circus. Mom was running around helping Karen get ready. It was mass confusion in the house. Dad was a nervous wreck. He had to get out of there. He finally decided to go to the church. Someone had to be there to meet the flowers when they arrived.

Mom told me to go with Dad. She said he would help me get ready when we got back. Actually, I think she just wanted me out from under foot. She had enough to do without having to watch after me every minute. I was relieved to get out of there for a while. Maybe things would be calmer when we returned.

I didn't see Karen again until the wedding. By the time Dad and I returned from the church, they were on their way there. Dad helped me put on my blue suit. I got a new pair of shoes just for the occasion. I thought I looked sleek.

The guests had started to arrive when Dad and I got back to the church. It was mostly family and some of Karen and Dean's friends. It was supposed to be a small ceremony, but by the time all of our family got together, there was quite a gathering.

Everything was arranged elegantly. The white and yellow flowers radiated the room. They gave our usually drab church parlor a new brilliance. It was sparkling. But nothing can compare in beauty to a bride. I never thought of my sister as beautiful before, but I saw her in a new light that day. She was stunning as she came down the aisle on Dad's arm.

I never realized how emotional weddings were. Mom choked back tears throughout the whole ceremony. She was losing her little girl. It was hard for her to let go. Then came the part of the ceremony where the preacher asked, "Do you take this man to love, honor and cherish?" I fought to keep from cracking up.

I looked over at my cousin. He looked like he wanted to laugh, too. Everybody was so busy looking at the bride and groom, I don't think anyone noticed us.

After the ceremony, I saw Dad take Dean aside and say something to him. I don't know what he said to him, probably one of those welcome-to-the family, take-care-of-my-daughter talks fathers give their future sons-in-law. And, too, he wanted Dean to know that he and Mom were there for them if they ever needed anything.

It was a joyous occasion. People were running around hugging each other. Some were laughing; Mom was crying. Finally, it was time for the newlyweds to be on their way.

Dean, fearful that some of our more deviant cousins might try to camouflage his pickup, had stowed the truck in a safe place. He kept the truck out of sight until it was time to leave. When it was time, Dean spun around to pick up Karen.

They jumped in the car and sped away, but not before we had a chance to shower them in rice. A couple of cousins tried to slip a string of tin cans on the back bumper before they got away, but they weren't quick enough. Dean helped Karen in the truck, and they were off.

There was a strange void in the house that night. It felt so empty. It felt as if Karen should come walking in any minute. Once, I turned to Mom and asked, "What time is Karen getting home tonight?" But she wasn't coming home. She was gone. She was really gone. It was just the three of us now.

Mom said it seemed as if Karen grew up and left too soon. "There are so many things I didn't get to tell her, so many things I didn't get to teach her," Mom said. "Who's going to show her these things?"

It took some getting used to her being gone. For days after the wedding, Mom found herself trying to remember to set only three plates at the dinner table instead of four. She would go into Karen's room, which was my room now, to tell her something, only to remember that she wasn't there. It was strange for all of us, but it was especially tough for Mom.

Mothers are like that. They don't want to let go. Thank God they never do.

So Little Patience

I had little patience as a young boy, and what little patience I had only seemed to dwindle the older I got. I hated waiting. I wanted to have everything right then, immediately.

The summer before I started high school seemed to last an eternity. Karen was out of the house and on her own now. Mom worked all day, and Dad was preoccupied with his new found interest in a backyard vegetable garden. I found myself searching for things to fill the wearisome days of summer.

The sizzling, summer sun stayed out longer and longer, making the days drag by. One day ran into the next. I didn't know what to do with myself and began to long for school to start.

I was anxious about starting high school. It was a big step. Like my first staggering steps across the kitchen linoleum, high school was one step Mom and Dad weren't sure I'd ever take. They had watched my progress cautiously. They hoped I would go on and graduate but still took nothing for granted. Each tiny step was a giant leap toward achieving independence.

I was especially nervous about starting high school. No longer would I be under Dad's watchful eye as I was in junior high. Dad wouldn't be there to catch me when I fell either. I had to stand on my own.

I could hardly wait for school to begin. Every day for two weeks I watched and waited for the mail, anticipating the arrival of my class schedule. I sat in the sweltering heat for hours at a time until I saw the postman inching his way up the street. My eyes traced his steps as he wound his way up the other side of the street, then crossed over and doubled back toward our house.

The excitement mounted the closer he got. Every day, I knew that would be the day. And each day my hopes were dashed as he brought bills, a department store circular or a Ladies Home Journal but no class schedule.

Then, one day in early August, it came. A bright yellow envelope. I knew what it was the minute I saw it. The mailman barely had laid loose of the envelope before I snatched it up. "It's here!" I screamed grabbing it and running into the house.

I ripped open the envelope, my heart pounding as my eyes ran down the slate of courses. It was all the usual freshman classes — history, science, math and English. Still, there was something about starting high school that made it more exciting.

That night, my best friend Bill came over, and we compared schedules. It was hard to tell who was more excited, Bill or me. I had hoped that we would have at least one class together. Although, it was probably better that we weren't in the same classes. After comparing schedules, we could hardly wait until the first day of school. We had to go look over the campus and find our classes.

Bill's mom thought we were silly. "It's not *that* big," she said. "You can't possibly get lost." But we had to see for ourselves. Bright and early the next day, we set out on our bicycles, Bill on his 10-speed and me on my three-wheeler.

It was the hottest day of summer as we rode to the high school. Or it seemed like it, anyway. It wasn't far, only eight blocks, but in 90-degree heat and the sweltering Texas south wind, we were sweating profusely when we arrived.

The building was empty, except for a handful of teachers preparing for the opening day of school. It was hauntingly eerie standing in the halls of the timeworn old building. It was a three-story building that stretched three city blocks. Standing at one end of the hall, I could hardly make out the insignia of the school mascot emblazoned above the entrance at the other end.

The building's multi-level design made it difficult for me to get around. As Bill and I roamed the halls searching for our classes, we had to climb the stairs several times. It was a struggle getting up the steep stairs.

Mom and Dad had worried about me climbing the stairs. They thought I might fall and tumble down the stairs or that someone would knock me over. Dad had thought a lot about it and tried to do something about it before I even got to high school.

Dad took on the school board in hopes of getting an elevator installed. He simply couldn't believe they had gone that long without an elevator. There were other students who needed it far worse than I did.

I was one of the lucky ones. At least I could climb the steps. Some couldn't use the stairs at all and had to attend classes in another part of the building. It made no sense at all to Dad. There had to be something he could do, he swore.

But the wheels of progress turn slowly, and it would be two more years before we would see an elevator become a reality. In the meantime, I had to battle the stairs.

The counselors knew it was hard for me to go up and down the stairs between classes, so they scheduled all my morning classes on the second floor and my afternoon classes on the first floor. It saved a lot of steps and precious energy only having to climb the stairs once a day.

I had no trouble with the steps that day with Bill. We wandered around the building nearly an hour, locating all of our classrooms and went up the stairs several times.

I never admitted it to anyone, but deep down, I was nervous about starting a new school and not knowing what the future held for me in high school.

The closer it got to the opening bell, the more anxious I became. Despite my achievements in junior high, I still had doubts, secretly wondering if I could really make it in high school. Low self-confidence haunted me and kept me from believing I could have a normal life. I was terrified. By the time the first day of school rolled around, I was so nervous I had a knot in the pit of my stomach.

A hundred questions ran through my mind when I thought about starting school. What if I can't handle it? What if I fail? It was only natural to have doubts. But it was that inept fear that made me more determined than ever to succeed.

It was strange the first day. Dad walked me to my first class and helped me up the stairs, still afraid I would fall climbing the steep steps. Then, he headed back to his school, and I was on my own.

Even though I had been there with Bill just the week before, I felt lost. The grades weren't divided as they were in junior high. The students all mixed in together in the halls, and there were some big kids in the halls, huge kids. I felt out of place but believed God would help me. He had brought me this far. Through faith, I would make it.

The first day, a bulky football player bumped into me in the hall. I dropped my books when he brushed me with his shoulder. He must have been a senior because he towered over me by a head.

I left class five minutes early but didn't make it to my next class before the bell rang and everyone started pouring into the hall. I tried to move to the side when he bumped me. I swerved to catch my balance and managed to keep from falling. It was only a slight nudge, but enough of a jolt to make me drop my books. He never even saw little me. He just plowed through and never looked back.

It was a long walk to some of my classes, and I couldn't always make it in the five minutes between classes. The school nurse loaned me a wheelchair, and I used it for the first few days, but once again it wasn't long before I abandoned the wheelchair and walked everywhere.

It was little things like walking and carrying my books that were the biggest hindrances. I had two lockers, one on each floor. It saved time, and I didn't have to lug books up the stairs.

Dad coerced one of the teachers into walking me down the stairs at noon. I was embarrassed having a teacher walk me down the stairs. I thought I could do it by myself, but Dad felt better if someone was with me. The stairways were always packed at noon. Most students were gracious and let me pass, but there were a few who tried to block my path.

With my inflexible muscles and stiff joints, I still couldn't do the rigorous activities of a gym class. I felt incomplete by never having gym. Besides the physical training that goes on, there's also the bonding and growing that takes place in the locker room as boys turn into men.

There's something about walking around a locker room with a bunch of sweaty guys in towels. And the talk that goes on. I missed all that.

While all the boys were in gym, I spent the last hour of each day studying in the library. The library was one of the few rooms that was air-conditioned. The cooled air hit me across the face as I walked into the library, and I melted into a chair and didn't move from that spot.

It had been a tiring first day, but a triumphant one. I had done something many thought I'd never do. I made it through my first day of high school, and even though I had lingering doubts, I was determined that I was going to make it.

High school was everything I expected it to be. There was greater freedom to discover my own beliefs and test my values. And along with freedom came more responsibility. Teachers didn't coddle students. They were there to teach, and it was up to the students to learn.

Teachers didn't pamper students by constantly reminding them to turn in their homework. It was expected. Certainly, they had to do some coaxing from time to time. But, ultimately, it was the student's decision to study and do the work.

High school was harder than junior high. I had to spend more time studying just to make a 'B' in high school. I knew grades were my only hope for making a life for my-self when I finished school, for getting a job and for realiz-ing my dream — to make it on my own.

I spent hours at a time studying, hoping the hard work would pay off. That's something Dad tried to instill in me: "If you work hard and always do your best, the extra effort will pay off in the end."

My parents pushed me to move beyond what I knew I could do and be the best I could be. One teacher especially encouraged me to take tougher courses that forced me to think and to grow. Beth Shannon taught freshman science. She took a special interest in me that year. She took an inter-est in all her students. That's the kind of teacher she was.

I knew Beth from church. I had grown up around her practically, so I was thrilled when I got in her class.

Beth was a devout Christian woman, and she continu-ally looked for ways to share her faith. She always tried to inlay something about God into her lessons.

She had a sign on the door of her room. At the top it gave a long, scientific formula for creating light, and then underneath it simply read: "And God said let there be light."

Even if it was just a phrase or a word, she tried to inject something every day to let God come through. It was al-ways very subtle. She never forced her beliefs on anyone.

Our science class that year studied the theory of evo-lution, the belief that species can change over a long pe-riod of time so that their descendants become less like their ancestors.

Beth craftfully included her belief in creationism, the story of man's origin as told in Genesis which says God created the heavens and the earth. She took a real chance by bringing religion into the lesson at a time when people were trying to expel God from the classroom. But she couldn't let the opportunity pass without sharing her belief in God.

I admired her for her strong beliefs. It was an inspiration to me at a time when I was testing my own faith. In those years as a confused, muddled-headed teen-ager, I fought with my faith. I wondered who is God? Where is God?

Mom had made me sit in church and listen to sermon after sermon from the time I was big enough to see over the pew. I was taught that God was a kind god, a caring god. Still, I couldn't help but wonder how such a loving god could allow such suffering.

Mom told me if I prayed to God, someday he would make me like everyone else. I believed that he would hear me, so for months on end I diligently prayed, "God, make me like other children so I am not different." Then, I waited patiently for him to answer my prayers.

I believed there was a purpose, though I didn't understand it for a long time. I continued to go to church and pray, but I wasn't living a godly life. I rebelled against God for a time as I searched to find answers about my life.

Seeing Beth share her love for others inspired me to look deeper within myself to find who God wanted me to be. It was in that science class that I found God again.

Besides strengthening my faith, Beth encouraged me to work hard and apply myself. She helped me to see that God only helps those who help themselves.

When Beth found out I was taking a basic math class instead of regular algebra, she tried to get me to take a more challenging class. She tried to get me to switch to regular algebra, but I was afraid to try. I took the easy way out. I was afraid to set higher stakes, afraid I would fail. Math was my worst subject. I could never see where algebra would ever help me in life.

Beth was disappointed I didn't challenge myself by taking the tougher class. It was the only time I remember a teacher telling me she was disappointed in me. Beth said something once that stuck with me: "A lot of people have the ability. But many never use it." I never forgot those words.

I discovered the truth in her words when I found myself in a remedial history class later that year. Basic classes taught the same material, but at a slower pace. They were meant to help students who needed a little extra time to learn. I got into the class quite by accident.

I had to take a health class the second half of my freshman year. That meant changing my schedule. The counselors tried to keep all my morning classes on the second floor, but the only open health class in the morning was on the third floor.

They tried to keep me off the third floor completely, so the only way around it was to put me in a basic history class. Dad was vehemently opposed to the idea. He agreed with Beth that I should take more advanced courses, but there was no other way.

The class wasn't much different from my regular history class. The same teacher taught both courses and covered the same material. It was actually more interesting because we spent more time talking about the events that shaped our country's history. It made history come to life. It became more than just names and dates.

I couldn't see that the class was that much easier until it came time for the first test. The exam consisted of 10 multiple-choice questions, and that was it. I got my test and finished it in less than five minutes. I was the first one finished.

I was usually the last one to turn in my test. It wasn't that I didn't know the answers, but it just took more time to write the answers on tests that were usually essay questions. On a multiple-choice test, I finished in no time.

After I turned in my paper, I looked around the room at the other students in the class. They were struggling over those simple questions. It was then that I realized I didn't belong in that class. It was like in junior high when they put me in special ed. It was easier, but I didn't belong there.

I made an 'A' in the class, but it didn't mean as much as 'A's I made in other classes. The class wasn't a challenge. I realized what Beth meant when she said a lot of people have a special gift, but they don't use it for good. It is wasted.

That was my first and only basic class because I knew I could do better. It was then I decided that I was going to take tougher classes, take a risk, challenge myself, even if it meant working harder, because in the end, I knew it would all be worth it.

Sticks and Stones

I always felt sheltered in school, safe from the chiding by other kids. My friends, some who had been around me since grade school, helped me when I needed it. They had been around me. They knew me and accepted me.

When I got to high school, I encountered a new group. I was afraid they wouldn't accept me. Something happens as people get older that makes them less trusting and less approving of others.

Most of the students I met were kind and tried to get to know me. But there were always the few people who never would accept me. They would never like me because I was different. They didn't say they didn't like me. They didn't have to. I knew the jokes they whispered as I passed in the hall, the snickers they made, and it hurt. If they would only take the time to see that I'm not all that different.

I was in the cafeteria one day, and a group of boys was talking and laughing at a table behind me.

It must have been the reporter's instinct in me that made me strain to hear their conversation. I had a habit of sticking my nose in places it didn't belong. But this time, I was sorry I did.

I was sitting with my back to the boys, and they hadn't noticed me sitting there. I couldn't make out everything they said, but I heard them talking about the freaks they let in school here.

"They can't even walk straight," one of them snarled.

My heart sank as I realized they were talking about me and Timmy, my friend from junior high who also had cerebral palsy. Two of the boys in the group were in the same geography class that Timmy and I were in. I remember them looking at me kind of strange, but I never gave it much thought until then.

All this time, they had been making fun of me and I didn't even realize it. How could I not have known they were talking about me? How could I have been so naive? I was getting angrier the longer I sat there. I didn't want to believe they were talking about me.

Finally, I had heard enough. I couldn't remain silent any longer. I whipped around in my chair and looked straight at them. My stare pierced them, silencing their conversation. They quickly got up and left without saying a word. They only snickered as they passed my table.

I just sat there, unable to move. I knew people made fun of me, but I never had encountered the chiding directly and it caught me off guard. I wondered how anyone could be so cruel. They didn't know me. They didn't know anything about me.

After that, whenever I saw those boys in class, they never said a word about that day in the cafeteria. They just turned their heads and looked away. I don't know if they ever realized what they had done. I like to think they realized what they did was wrong and tried to make it right.

I knew there always would be people like that in the world. It's ignorance that keeps people from understanding. I felt sorry for them. I really did. They would never have the chance to know someone like Timmy or me.

Schoolboy Crush

L ike any other 15-year-old, I was growing more, both
physically and emotionally. My voice started cracking.
As if my speech wasn't already garbled enough, now my
voice squeaked every time I said anything. I sounded like
I had a whistle stuck in my throat. My face started sprout-
ing hair, and I had to start shaving once a week, which
created quite another problem.

I had entered the confusing age of puberty.

I noticed girls were changing, too. They were different.
They weren't different in the way I was different from able-
bodied people, but they were definitely different. There
were curves in places where there had been none.

Biology class and studying the reproductive system only
helped to pique my interest in the opposite sex. We had
biology lab twice a week. The teacher split the class into
teams of four people each. I was in a group with three
girls: Sonya West, Karen Anderson and Bonita Rogers.

They were all a year younger than me. Even though it
was a sophomore class, there was a mix of freshmen and
sophomores in the class.

I had a huge crush on Sonya. Sonya was the brightest girl in the class, and one of the prettiest I thought. She had wavy curves in all the right places. I couldn't help notice them when she leaned in to look at a slide under the microscope. But that wasn't what attracted me to her. It was the way she made me feel whenever she was around.

Sonya made me feel special, like I mattered. It was the little things she said and did to show she cared about me. On Valentine's Day that year, she sent me a Kiss-o-gram. It was a card decorated with paper hearts, brightly colored ribbons and a chocolate-candy Kiss placed in one corner.

The home economics classes made the cards and sold them after school. All the boys got one for their sweethearts and inscribed a love note on the card.

Those who were too timid to reveal their true intentions sent cards anonymously. I never paid much attention to them because I didn't have a girlfriend, and I never expected anyone to send me one. It came as quite a shock when they came around in homeroom delivering the notes.

Several girls in my homeroom received one, then they called my name. It caught me so by surprise. I couldn't imagine who would be sending me a Kiss-o-gram. Sonya was a friend, but I never really professed her as my girlfriend. I would have gladly admitted I was crazy about her, but I didn't know if she felt the same about me.

I got a warm feeling inside when I read the card and saw Sonya's name. I felt my heart doing flips. "Hope your heart is full of love. Happy Valentine's Day. Sonya," she inscribed on the card.

My heart was full of love that day because someone cared enough about me to send me a card. I felt bad I didn't have anything for her. When I saw Sonya later that afternoon in biology class and thanked her for the card, I apologized for not giving her anything.

"But you have given me something," she said warmly.

I thought for a minute. I couldn't remember ever giving her anything.

"You gave me your friendship," she said.

That's when I discovered the true meaning of Valentine's Day. It's about friendship and showing those you care about how much they mean. Sonya had done that. She had shown me she cared.

Sonya and I became closer friends after that. We never were actually a couple. I had accepted the fact that I probably wouldn't have many girlfriends. That was all right. It was all right just being friends. Friendships can be the most special relationships.

I cherished the time we had together. Sonya played in the school band. I loved to go listen to her play. The band performed at half-time at home basketball games. I never was a sports fan. Most of the time I didn't know what the score was, but I could sit and listen to Sonya play for hours.

I could pick out Sonya's horn above everybody else in the band. She made that horn sing. I went to so many band performances people thought I was part of the band. I felt like I was part of the band.

At the end of the year, Sonya asked me to the band's end-of-school banquet. It was a gala event every year. The boys rented tuxedoes, and the girls got new formal dresses. It was almost as big as the prom, and Sonya asked me to be her escort.

I was thrilled when Sonya asked me. I couldn't believe she wanted me to take her. But I turned her down. It's not that I didn't want to go. I wanted more than anything to take her, but I just couldn't. I had only danced once in my life, and that was at the Lions Club's camp. I felt silly then, and I was certain I'd look silly if I tried to dance now.

No one understood why I didn't want to go. Mom said we could rent a tuxedo for the dance. I told Sonya I couldn't go because we were having company and my parents wouldn't let me go.

I couldn't tell her the real reason I wouldn't go. The truth was I liked Sonya too much to go with her. I didn't want to embarrass her in front of her friends. I was afraid if I went and tried to dance, I'd trip and look like a clumsy fool. Sonya still didn't understand why I wouldn't go. She sensed there was another reason, but she didn't force me.

The closer the night of the dance got, the more I wanted to call Sonya and tell her I changed my mind. I wanted to tell her I'd go, but I couldn't. It just wasn't right.

The night of the banquet I sat home alone. I was miserable. I kept thinking about Sonya. After I told her I couldn't go, she asked someone else. I thought about them all night. I wondered what they were doing, if they were having a good time. It was the longest night of my life — and the loneliest.

I knew it didn't matter to Sonya that I couldn't dance. She didn't care if I was a bumbling fool. She liked me the way I was, but I missed my chance.

School let out the week after the banquet, and I didn't see Sonya much during the summer. When school started the next year, we didn't have any classes together, and we lost track of each other. I saw her in the hall once in a while, and I'd talk to her but it was never the same.

I'd always been one for taking chances. I believed I'd never get anything in life unless I tried. I didn't try, and I lost out. Chances are nothing would have changed if I had gone to the dance that night. But there's always that one chance that things might have been different. If only I'd stepped out and taken a chance.

Driving

〜

Summers were the loneliest time of year for me. The days were filled with many long, empty hours. That's the reason I slept late in the summer.

Sometimes, I felt as if I was cheating myself out of part of life by not making use of that time. When I made myself get up, usually around 10, I spent most of the day inside under the air conditioner and in front of the television.

There wasn't a lot for a boy without a summer job or a car to do in a small West Texas town, and I had neither.

The summer between my sophomore and junior years looked to be even more solitary. Bill wasn't around as much that summer. We were usually inseparable in the summer, taking cross-town bike rides, camping out in the back yard or just sitting under a shade tree, but that year Bill went to work at his granddad's gas station, fixing flats and pumping gas.

I was lost without Bill. I'd always had a friend to run around with in Bill, and now he was gone.

The only hope I saw in saving the summer from complete boredom was that it was the summer before my 16th birthday. Sixteen is a coming of age. It is the age of first loves. It often is the age of a first kiss.

There was another rite of passage in turning 16. It was the age of discovering the freedom of the road when most teens get driver's licenses.

I had dreamed how it would be when I got my license. I had it all figured out. There were driving classes every fall and summer at the high school. I figured I could take driver's ed that summer, then when my birthday rolled around in October, I'd take the test and get my license.

I watched the newspaper every day, waiting for an announcement of when the driving classes would start. When it finally came out, I rode my bicycle to the school to sign up.

As I rode, I thought about how wonderful it would be when I got my license. I could drive to school. I could go to the mall by myself. I'd be able to go anywhere!

I picked up a registration form in the office and started home. I kept thinking that soon I wouldn't have to pedal everywhere I went. I'd have a car. I still had to have Mom or Dad sign the form, but I figured once I got their OK, I'd be on the road to freedom.

I never thought it would be so complicated and bring so much heartache getting there.

Mom was in the kitchen frying a chicken when I got home with the papers.

"I need you to sign this," I said laying the paper on the counter.

"What is it?" she asked.

"It's just a form I have to fill out for driver's ed. All you have to do is sign it," I said, pushing the paper a little closer.

"Wait a minute. Driver's ed?"

"Yes, I have to take it this summer so I can get my license by my birthday."

"I don't know, Chris," she said turning a piece of chicken over in the skillet. "I think you better talk to your dad about this."

"What's there to talk about?" I asked, starting to get flustered.

"Well, I'm not sure if you're going to be able to get a license."

"Why not?" I demanded. I was really starting to get worked up now. I hadn't considered the possibility that I wouldn't get my license. Dad had taken me out and let me drive on country roads in the old Plymouth he drove back and forth to work. Now to think that I wouldn't be able to drive, I couldn't imagine it.

"We'll just have to wait and see," Mom continued. "I don't know if you can handle that."

Dad came around the corner about that time, probably smelling the chicken frying. Dad was always the first one to the table.

"There's your father. Talk to him about it," Mom said.

"Talk to me about what?" he asked hesitantly.

"Your son wants to take driving. I told him he had to talk to you."

Dad was silent. For a minute, I thought he was going to be on my side and that he would tell Mom that I could handle it. After all, he was the one who always tossed me the keys and told me to back the car out of the driveway and park it in the street. For a brief second, I had a glimmer of hope. Then, suddenly, my hopes came crashing down.

"Son, they're not going to let you have a driver's license," he said.

"Why not?" I asked. My voice started quivering and tears welled up in my eyes. "Why won't they give me a license?"

"I really don't think you can handle driving a car," he said.

"It's not fair! You let me drive in the country. Just let me try."

"No!" he said sternly. "I'm sorry. Not now." And with that the discussion came to an abrupt end. I burst into tears and bolted from the room.

I ran to my room and slammed the door. I was furious. Why wouldn't they at least let me try?

My anger turned to rage. I went into a tantrum. I took my arm and with one sweep, brushed everything on the dresser off into the floor. I pounded my fist against the floor, but all that did was make my hand throb. I couldn't understand why my parents were treating me so unfairly.

I lost my balance trying to upset the things on my desk, and my shoe came off. It incensed me even more. I picked up the shoe and threw it against the door, then fell limp in the floor crying.

Mom tried to get me to come out and eat, but I wasn't hungry, which was unusual for me. I usually wanted to eat all the time, but I couldn't eat now. Mom tried to explain why they couldn't let me take driving. She said she knew I could drive, but they were concerned that my reflexes wouldn't be quick enough to make sudden stops. She said my muscles weren't strong enough to steady a car.

I didn't understand. I thought they were being cruel. I thought it was unfair. Life was unfair. Mom tried to persuade me to come out of my room and eat. I didn't want to eat. I wanted to stay in there and feel sorry for myself. I had a right to feel sorry for myself, and I wanted to pity myself.

I stayed in my room the rest of the night, trying to find a way to convince them I could do it. I calmed down gradually, but there were occasional outbursts of anger. It was then that I started questioning God. I wanted to know why. Why was this happening to me?

I cried out to God. I was angry at God and at life. I blamed him. "Why me?" I kept asking him. "Why did this have to happen to me, God? Why?"

It was natural, I guess, to want to know why, but until then it was a question I never thought to ask. I accepted my disability as part of life, the nature of things. Life wasn't always fair. I had accepted that. I never had blamed God.

I believed there must be a reason for all things. "For by him all things were created: things in heaven and on earth, visible and invisible, whether thrones or powers or authorities, all things were created by him and for him," Colossians 1:16 said. I believed God created me for a purpose. He had a purpose in making me the way he did. But I also believed in God's power to change things. I believed in miracles.

Mom and Grandma Altman had prayed and asked God for a miracle. I can't count the number of times they prayed for me. I remember my mom and my Sunday school teacher taking me to a healing crusade in Amarillo when I was about 10 years old. They prayed that God would heal me.

Everyone prayed for me that night. I had so many hands on me I felt like a rag doll that everybody just passed around. I didn't understand why I wasn't healed because I knew it was possible. Even at that young age, I believed it was possible.

I lay in bed that night after everyone had gone to sleep, and with tears streaming down my face, I called out to God.

"Why is life unfair?" I cried. "Why has life dealt me this hand?" I really felt sorry for myself. I prayed for a miracle.

That night, I felt God would either have to heal me or reveal his purpose for making me that way. God didn't answer me that night, or at least it wasn't the answer I wanted. I finally cried myself to sleep.

I sulked for days afterward, moping around the house. I thought if I sulked long enough, Mom and Dad would have to give in and let me take driver's ed, but my efforts were to no avail. They tried to help me to understand it was because they loved me, but, of course, I didn't understand.

I continued to search for the answers about my life, but I no longer blamed God. I sought him and his purpose for my life. God is a loving god. I knew he had a plan and that if I just looked to him, in time, his purpose would reveal itself.

My Calling

≈

God doesn't follow man's timetable, yet his timing proved itself to me time and time again. It may not have seemed like it, but God had a plan. There were times in my life where God clearly was leading my steps, even though I didn't realize it at the time.

One of the biggest heartbreaks in life was trying to accept the harsh reality that I wouldn't get my driver's license when I turned 16. All my friends were driving and experiencing the freedom of the open road. I never once stopped to consider that I might not be able to operate a machine that required such exact coordination.

It made me look to my future. What else wouldn't I be able to do? I had thought about the future, but I never thought about what I wanted to do after high school. I dreamed about going to college, but I wasn't sure if I would be able to go. More and more, I began seeking God's direction for my life.

When school started that fall, God's plan began to become clear, but it came in a way that I was unaware it was even happening.

I couldn't take the usual array of virile classes that were popular with boys — wood shop and auto mechanics. Each year, Dad and I sat down and tried to figure out which classes I would be able to take.

Dad always suggested classes that would make me think. Classes like psychology and anatomy. When I made out my schedule at the end of my sophomore year, I needed one class as an alternate in case my first choice for electives filled up. The high school counselor suggested journalism.

I knew little about journalism or newspapers, but I liked to write so I decided to try it. Besides, the counselor assured me the chances of having to actually use my alternate schedule were slim.

Sure enough, when I received my schedule a few weeks before school started, the first thing on it was journalism. I was nervous about the class because, although I liked the idea of crafting stories, I shied away from anything that involved a lot of handwriting.

I did all right if I had a typewriter, but at the time, the school newspaper had only one typewriter and there weren't many computers when I was in school. Budding reporters had to write their stories longhand, then use a typesetter to set the stories into print.

I was terrified about the class at first, but my fears vanished as I learned about journalism and newspapers. I quickly became fascinated by journalism. I realized later it was no coincidence that those other classes were full and I wound up in journalism.

It was God's way of leading me. It was the first step in a sequence of events that led me to a career in journalism. It was clearly God's hand working in my life, guiding me in his way.

I wasn't alone in sharing my reluctance about taking the class. The journalism teacher, Lynda Queen, was concerned about me taking the class.

Journalism is a talking-intensive business, and because of my speech, Mrs. Queen wondered if I would be able to communicate well enough to do the interviews. But she welcomed me into the class anyway and gave me a chance.

We didn't start writing right away. We studied the advent of the printing press and the first daily newspaper in the American colonies, the Pennsylvania Evening Post, in 1783. It seemed more like a history class than a writing course.

I never was that fond of history, but I found it interesting, especially the early-day journalists — William Randolph Hearst and Benjamin Day and the publishers of the penny papers — I wanted to be just like them. But the thing that brought it to life for me was when I got to see the workings of an actual newspaper.

Mrs. Queen took the class on a tour of *The Pampa News*. It was a small daily and the only newspaper I'd ever read. We wandered around the newsroom, watching reporters scrambling around the room on deadline, and we saw the presses roll.

I was captivated by the whole operation, seeing a story start with an idea and watching it blossom into a finished story and then finding its way onto the pages of the newspaper.

I had all these thoughts inside of me, but because of my speech, I had no way to express my feelings. After seeing the newspaper, I knew I was meant to be a newspaperman.

After several weeks of studying the history of journalism, my hands were itching to write. Mrs. Queen started me off slow. My first assignment was to write a story about the school's new elevator.

The school board, after years of stalling, saw the light and went to work on getting an elevator at the high school.

It was installed over the summer, and it was ready when school opened in the fall. It was a small elevator, and only students with a disability or students who were injured were permitted to use it.

Mrs. Queen asked me to write the story because she thought who better to write about it than someone who actually would be using the elevator. It was a rather crude story. I hardly knew how to go about writing a news story. I had written narratives about my family and make-believe stories about adventures I dreamed of having, but this was different.

I agonized over it for days. Finally, I sat down and started writing. I told how the elevator would help students who broke their legs, saving precious steps up and down the stairs. The elevator got quite a workout during football season, when players hurt their legs and were unable to climb the stairs.

The article wasn't completely objective because the elevator was meant to help me, after all.

It was a tiny elevator, only about the size of a broom closet. It was barely big enough for three people to ride comfortably. It shook like a roller coaster when it moved. I was more than a little bit leery of riding it. I tried to avoid elevators altogether. I'd rather walk up 10 flights of stairs than ride the elevator. I just knew it would get stuck.

Sure enough, the second time I got on it, the thing that I was afraid would happen happened. The elevator got stuck.

I had gotten on the elevator after school one day when it got stuck between floors. I was in there only about 20 minutes, but it seemed like hours. It was smoldering in the cramped space. There was no breeze at all. It must have been 100 degrees in there. I broke out in a sweat. I was frightened. I thought I was going to be in there all night.

I finally was freed when Dad came to pick me up and I wasn't outside waiting. He knew something was wrong and came in looking for me. When he didn't see me in the hall, Dad decided to check in the office.

Dad decided to check the elevator on the way to the office. That's when he heard me. Dad alerted the office, and they were able to start the elevator with a crank in the basement. They had me out within minutes.

The elevator was out of service for several days while they tried to repair the problems, which was perfectly all right with me. I swore I would never ride that thing again. Dad convinced me to give it another chance. He reminded me that they put in the elevator to help me, so I should try to use it. I was still a little reluctant but finally agreed to give it another chance.

My story omitted the details of my harrowing experience, except to say the elevator left a couple of riders stranded early in the year. The story was sketchy on all accounts. It was all of four paragraphs.

I asked Dad to read the story before I turned it in. He offered some constructive criticism, which no writer likes to hear but invariably must accept. He suggested a few changes, which I admit improved the article, although it was still pretty rough.

The story went through more changes before it appeared in the paper the next week — the power of an editor. I was so proud the first time I saw my words in print.

You would have thought I had written a Pulitzer-prize winner. I thought I really had accomplished something getting my story in the paper, and I had. Or at least it was a start.

A Budding Reporter

If I was going to be a reporter, I needed a beat. We drew lots, and everyone in the class got an assignment. Mrs. Queen wrote the names of the beats on slips of paper, and everyone drew one.

Some reporters snagged a newsy beat: student government, the debate team, the drama department. Others of us weren't as lucky. I got stuck with the cafeteria beat.

Besides writing how bland the food was, I wondered what I could possibly find to write about the cafeteria. I was stymied.

I talked to the cafeteria manager each week in search of a scoop, and for the first couple of weeks, I came up with a story. After a few weeks, though, I began running out of ideas and started venturing into other areas for stories. My reporter's instincts led me to a history teacher who had worked in politics before turning to teaching.

I was in her American history class and was fascinated by the stories she told about working for the campaigns of a president and a former governor. I told the editor,

Patt Richards, about her, and he asked me to write a story about her.

I interviewed Miss Spearman after school one day and found out she was a field coordinator for President Reagan's re-election campaign. She arranged visits for George Bush, then the vice president, when he was campaigning in Texas, and she helped with the president's fund-raisers. She also had worked for a senator and a governor.

I was astounded by the people she knew. It made for an interesting story, all the notable people and even a notorious criminal. Miss Spearman said in her college days, she knew John Hinkley Jr., the man who shot President Reagan.

I conducted the interview in a somewhat crude fashion. I wrote my questions on a piece of notebook paper, and Miss Spearman read along because it was difficult for her to understand me.

Then, she wrote down her responses to make it easier for me to record her answers. It may not have been the customary way to interview someone, but it was the best way I knew to communicate. I couldn't interview the normal way, so I had to adapt.

I gleaned a glimmer of light into Miss Spearman's life from the interview, and I worked on the story for two weeks to get everything right. I worked harder on it than any story I'd written. It had to be perfect. I battled over every word, trying to choose just the right phrase.

I finished the story and turned it in to the editor. It wasn't flawless, but it gave me a sense of pride, knowing that I had worked so hard to get a story. Patt raved over it.

Mrs. Queen was rather surprised by it. Neither she nor Patt had really expected any more out of me, so they hadn't given me challenging stories. They looked at me differently after that, though. I got better assignments once they saw what I could do.

Mrs. Queen encouraged me to write more. I wrote features on other teachers and profiles on students. I relished over writing stories. It became my passion.

I turned from features to writing news stories. Mrs. Queen worked with me after school to help me improve my stories. She believed in me and my writing ability. My writing improved during the year, and Mrs. Queen convinced me to compete in the interscholastic newswriting contest that spring.

The contest was the literary equivalent of the University Interscholastic League competition for sports. I never had competed in anything in my life. I scarcely paid any attention to UIL until Mrs. Queen asked me to compete. I didn't really realize the prominence placed on the contest, or I probably would have been too nervous to compete. I simply saw it as a way to get out of school for a day.

The contests lasted all day at West Texas State University. Pampa took a busload of students, 36 in all, competing in science, math, typing, journalism and spelling.

As I boarded the big, Harvester bus, painted in the school colors of green and gold, for the first time, I felt like I was part of a team. I was excited about competing against other students in the district, but I really didn't know what to expect.

While the other Pampa students roamed the campus before their contests, Mrs. Queen took her students, about seven of us, to the library for some last-minute preparation.

She tried to reassure us. "You're all going to do great," she said. Mrs. Queen was the kind of teacher who was always jovial and cheery.

Newswriting was the first contest. I was relieved that I was going first. I could go in and be done with it. I was nervous, but Mrs. Queen assured me I could do it.

The contest was timed, which made it more difficult for me. No allowance was given for my handicap. I was expected to compete like any other student. I wasn't looking for favors. I wanted to be treated the same as everybody else, but I thought if I could type my story, I could finish in the same time it took everyone else to handwrite theirs. And I thought the judges would be able to read it easier.

My handwriting was illegible when I got in a hurry. It was shaky anyway, and when I tried to hurry it only made it worse. I thought if I could type it, the judges would be able to read it, but the judges refused to make an exception. They said it would distract the other contestants, me banging around on the keyboard. I would have to do the best I could in the time I had and hope for the best.

They gave each contestant a sheet of a paper with feign quotes and facts, and we had 45 minutes to write a story. I read the information sheet through twice carefully and tried to organize my story in my mind. I read through the sheet a third time and then started writing.

I strained to print each letter legibly, bearing down on my pencil so hard I broke the lead and had to ask for a new one. I wanted desperately for the judges to be able to read my writing, but I knew I had to hurry.

The test monitor strolled up to the blackboard every few minutes and wrote how much time was remaining. That made me more jittery. I had to hurry, I told myself. I was taking too much time. I had to speed up.

I read through the fact sheet once more and then began writing, weaving quotes with the rest of the information.

My handwriting got noticeably dimmer the closer it came to the deadline.

I was starting the last paragraph when the monitor announced time was up. "Put your pencils down and turn your papers over on your desks," she said. I wasn't finished yet. I needed more time! But that was it. I had to be satisfied with what I had. The monitor instructed us to leave our papers on the desks as we left.

Mrs. Queen was perched outside the door when I came out. "How do you think you did?" she asked in her usual cheery voice.

"I don't know," I said. "I didn't finish."

"I'm sure you did great," Mrs. Queen said, patting me on the shoulder. I honestly didn't know how I did. I thought I had done poorly because I didn't finish.

Now, I had to wait. The judges would grade the papers and post the winners precisely at 3 o'clock. It was 1:30 when I finished. I had an hour and a half before I learned the results. Meanwhile, the next contest was starting, and two of my classmates were competing.

I was too nervous to stay at the test site. I decided to roam around campus. As I made my way across the huge campus, I prayed that I had done all right in the contest. "God, please don't let me let Mrs. Queen down," I prayed. I didn't care if I was disappointed, but I didn't want to let Mrs. Queen down. She had worked so hard to help me.

Thirty minutes passed, then 45. Finally, I couldn't take it any longer. I started back. I thought by the time I got over there, the results might be out. I walked slowly, still fretting over how poorly I thought I had done.

The feature writing contest was letting out when I reached the site. Contestants lined the halls waiting for the results. The suspense was thick in the air. It was like a fog had formed in the hallway. Finally, a woman came out with a sheet of white paper.

Everyone started crowding around the door. I couldn't get in close enough. I couldn't see the results. Suddenly, I heard a loud squeal. Mrs. Queen had nudged her way through the mountainous crowd to the head of the line.

The crowd began to clear out, and I moved closer to where Mrs. Queen was standing. "Chris, you won! You won!" she exclaimed. "You got first place!" She grabbed me and gave me a big hug. "You won!" She was more excited than I was.

I was excited, but it hadn't sunk in yet. I was shocked.

Mrs. Queen was ecstatic. "We have to call your mom and tell her the news. You're going to regionals!" she said, pulling me closer for another hug. I didn't think I needed to call Mom, it being long distance and all, but Mrs. Queen insisted.

"You've got to give her the good news," she said.

She got Mom on the line and handed me the phone.

"Chris, what's wrong? Is something wrong?" Mom asked. "Where are you?"

"No, everything fine. I won. I won the contest," I said.

"You won?" She asked, sounding surprised.

"Yes. First place. I'm going to regionals."

"That's wonderful," she said, not sure how to react.

She was thrilled, of course, but I don't think she knew what to say. It was a surprise more than anything. I never thought I'd win. That thought never entered my mind. Mrs. Queen wasn't surprised, though. She told me I could do it. She believed in me.

Our class fared well in the rest of the day's contests. Three other journalism students also won, two in editorial writing and an alternate in headline writing. Four English students also won district, giving Pampa a strong contention for the regional contest.

I felt like an athlete must feel after winning a game. Exhausted, but invigorated. It was a great feeling. Pampa was the big winner that day with seven students advancing to regionals, and for the first time, I was part of the winning team.

The Competition

Regionals were the last weekend in April at Brownwood in Central Texas. That left three weeks after district contest to prepare. Mrs. Queen began drilling us immediately after returning from district.

It was hard to concentrate on school for thinking about my next feat. That's all I thought about for three weeks. Studying turned into drudgery the closer it came to the contest.

The end of school was a drag anyway. Warm weather was coming on. The days started getting longer, and I started getting spring fever. There were so many distractions the closer it got to the end of the year. This year it was worse. All I could think about was going to Regionals.

Mrs. Queen even found it hard to get back on track after we returned from the contest. She talked about it for days afterward, recounting how the Journalism 1 class dominated the contests.

She was more excited than any of us students who were competing, and understandably so. It was as much of an accomplishment for her as it was for the students.

She gave us more drills and practice tests. We worked long hours after school getting ready. Regionals were more competitive than district with only the top student journalists making the cut. Mrs. Queen told us competition would be stiff. I knew I had to be prepared.

I knew it would be a challenge, but it was one I had to take. I couldn't compete in sports. This was my chance to make my mark. I wanted it more than anything. I had to do this. I worked hard and I was ready when it came time to leave.

Students, teachers and the journalism staff turned out to give us a grand send-off. The principal gave each of us a green-and-gold key ring emblazoned with the school's emblem for luck. He told us we represented dear ol' Pampa High and were competing for its honor as well as our own. I felt privileged to be among that group.

At last, we were off. Seven students, two teachers, Ralph the bus driver and . . . my mother! That's right, Mom was tagging along. She insisted that I needed someone to go with me because I couldn't make the trip alone.

Mom and Dad were proud of me and they wanted me to go, but they didn't think I should go alone. I was sure I could, but Mom talked to Mrs. Queen and they thought it was best if Mom went along.

I was embarrassed at first, having my mother tag along on the most important trip of my life, but I didn't mind it too much. I was thrilled just to be going. Nothing could have kept me from getting on that bus.

You get to know people pretty well after spending six hours cramped in a car together. I already knew Patt

Richards, the editor of the paper, and I knew Marc Gilbert and Jessica Patton from journalism class.

Then, there was Kambra Winningham, the girl I had a crush on in fourth grade. Kambra was the brightest girl in the class even then. We had become close friends in the years since grade school.

Kambra and the other two people in our group, David McGrath and Traci Gibson, made up the contention in the English categories along with the English teacher, Mrs. Lockwood.

A few miles out of town, Patt quipped up and asked, "Are we there yet?" Then, Marc piped in: "I need to go to the bathroom!" Patt and Marc got it started, and soon everybody joined in. Everyone was laughing and joking. You wouldn't expect a trip with two teachers and your mother, nonetheless, to be fun, but it was.

We arrived in Abilene by nightfall and spent the night there before going on to Brownwood the next morning. The teachers wanted us to get plenty of rest before the contest, but no one slept much that night. Everyone was excited and nervous.

I stayed in the room with the other guys. We sat outside until late in the cool night air, bouncing a rubber ball off the motel balcony down on people below, then ducking back into the room. I was having the time of my life. I was one of the guys for the first time in my life, and I knew how to have fun with the best of them, joining in on their pranks.

A man checked into the room next to us. He was on his way to Dallas on a business trip and looked in dire need of a good night's sleep. Patt told him we'd try to keep the noise down.

The man was a good sport about it. "Don't worry about the noise," he said. "No one can keep me awake."

"Wanna bet?" I retorted after he was out of ear range. We finally had to go in when Mrs. Queen and Mrs. Lockwood came down and tried to get us to go to bed.

The next day started early. It was still an hour's drive to Brownwood. The contests didn't start until that afternoon, but we had to be there early to check in with the UIL officials.

It was much more subdued on the bus that morning. Everyone was getting nervous now. The closer we got, the more nervous everyone became. I could feel the muscles tightening up in my stomach. I was terrified. Mrs. Queen told us not to worry, just do our best, but I couldn't help but worry.

We arrived in Brownwood to get our contest assignments at the college shortly before 10. The contest schedule was the same as the district competitions, with newswriting first.

My contest began at 1, so we decided to look around campus before checking into the motel. The competitions were at Howard Payne University. It was a picturesque, little campus, nestled around a clump of towering Oaks.

I fantasized what it would be like to actually go to college, holding on to the hope that I would go to college — someday.

We found the room where the contests would take place in the communications complex. We looked around the newsroom, then headed to the motel for lunch.

I didn't have much of an appetite, which was unusual for me. My stomach was tied up in knots. I was too nervous to eat. Mom said I should try to eat something. She said I needed energy to help me in the contest and, as I soon found out, I would need all the energy I could muster.

I didn't think I'd be able to eat anything, but I managed to finish a cheeseburger and fries. Then, I went back to the room and tried to rest before it was time to leave. I wasn't a bit tired, though. I should have been exhausted because we didn't go to bed until after 2 that morning.

Mrs. Queen came and got me when it was time to go. "This is it," she said in her usual jovial voice. "Are you ready?"

"I think so," I said, trying to sound confident even if I wasn't.

Only Mom and Mrs. Queen went with me back to the college. The others stayed at the motel until it was time for their competitions. The journalism contests were all that day, while the English competition was the next day.

We arrived back at campus an half-hour before the bout got under way. That gave me time to get settled and psyched up. Mom had done pretty good at not mothering me too much on the trip, but she had to get sentimental when we pulled up in front of the school. She got all teary-eyed and mushy, then Mrs. Queen joined in. They both gave me big hugs and tried to reassure me before we went in.

No one else was there when we arrived. I went in and took a seat on the back row. The other students filed in slowly. Mom and Mrs. Queen stayed with me until they made the teachers leave. Finally, it was time to begin.

I was still nervous, but I knew what to expect this time. I had only 45 minutes, so I had to work fast. A gray-haired, wrinkled professor monitored the competition. She looked like an old schoolmarm. Her hair was tightly wound in a bun on top of her head, and she wore a pair of wire-rimmed glasses.

The old professor gave each student an information sheet and four pieces of blank paper. She held a stopwatch in her left hand ready to start the contest. The room was silent except for the ticking of the stopwatch. I heard the watch click, signaling us to begin. Everyone began shuffling papers on the desks and started writing.

I didn't waste a lot of time reading the material this time. I read completely through the information once, taking notes as I went along. I wasted little time crafting a lead. The lead would be the first thing the judges would see when they read my story. It had to be perfect.

When I had the lead the way I wanted it, I jumped right into the rest of the story. The story had the same fictitious characters and make-believe town as the story at district.

My eyes stayed fixed on the paper, glancing occasionally at the information sheet to add additional facts or pull a quote for the story. I never looked at the blackboard to see how much time remained. I kept writing. I had to finish this time.

I wrote as fast as I could. It was unbearably sticky in the room. I started perspiring as I pored over the story. I expended so much energy trying to print neatly and finish on time, I broke out in a deep sweat. My mouth was dry, and my breathing was irregular.

I wrote and wrote for what seemed like hours, although I knew it had to be less than an hour. I finally looked at the board. There were five minutes left. I was going to make it. I was going to finish! I barreled down again to get the last words on the paper.

I finished with a few minutes remaining. I skimmed over the story to make certain I hadn't left out any words. I still wasn't satisfied with the story, but there was no time to change it. I had to be content with it, even though I knew it wasn't as good as it should be.

The professor instructed us to leave our papers on the desks as we left the room. I came out of the room, my hair dripping with sweat. I felt as if I had just run a marathon. I was drained when I came out.

It really got to Mrs. Queen when she saw me. Mom started wiping my brow with a handkerchief. "Are you all right?" she asked. "You look exhausted."

I was exhausted, but it was a good exhaustion.

"I'm all right," I said. "I just need to sit down for a minute."

Mom guided me over to a bench, while Mrs. Queen went to get me a glass of water. The cool water soothed me, and I began to catch my breath again.

"How did it go in there?" Mrs. Queen asked after I'd had time to catch my breath.

"I could've done better if I'd had more time," I said. "I finished, but I know I could've done better."

"I'm sure you did great," she said. "You did your best, and that's all you can do now."

I was just relieved it was over. The van was waiting to take us back to the motel, then came the unbearable task of waiting again. The judges would post the results after all the contests that day. I decided I wasn't going to worry, that whatever happened happened, but it was hard to get it off my mind.

I lay down when I got back to the motel room. Patt and Marc had gone to their contest already, and only David was left in the room. I tried to take a nap but never could get to sleep. The muscle tightness began to ease as I lay there. I kept thinking about the story and what if I had written this differently or done that differently. It was easy to recreate the story in my mind after it was finished.

It was no use to try to sleep, so I decided to go for a walk. A mall sat just across a vacant field behind our motel, so I decided to walk over there while I was waiting. It might take my mind off the contest, I thought.

I started out, crossing the parking lot and cutting through the vacant field. I got half way through the field that was knee deep in tall grass and stickers and glanced over my shoulder toward the motel. David was on the balcony watching me. He probably wondered where I was going. I didn't tell anyone I was leaving. I just started out. I kept going and by the time I reached the other side, David had started across the field.

He ran to catch up to me. He was a fast runner and had no trouble catching me, but I wondered why he was coming after me. The others had gone over to the mall earlier, so I knew it was all right.

"What's wrong?" I asked when he had caught up with me. "Do they want me to come back?"

"No, I just wanted to go to the mall," he said.

Maybe he did want to go to the mall, but somehow I didn't think that was it. There was another reason. Everywhere I went in the mall, he stuck close by my side. It was obvious that he didn't think I should be there alone because I was disabled. He wouldn't admit that was the reason. He didn't have to. It was obvious.

David didn't say much. He just stayed a couple of feet behind me the whole time. I felt like a criminal being watched. His intentions were good, but his concern was unnecessary. I turned to him once and told him he didn't have to worry about me. I could take care of myself.

"I wasn't worried," he said.

I would have been glad if I thought he came because he wanted to be with me, but he came out of sympathy. He hardly knew me. He felt obligated to watch over me because no one else was there.

I didn't need sympathy. I needed a friend. If he had taken the time to get to know me, he would have seen that his concerns were unfounded. Instead, he assumed that because I was disabled I needed someone to go with me. It didn't help matters that my mom was along on the trip.

David stayed close by all the time we were in the mall, then walked me back to the motel. I wanted to say something to him but didn't know how. I shrugged it off, hoping that someday people would see me for who I really was, and not who they thought I was.

When I got back, the van was waiting to take Mom and me back to the college to find out the contest results. The jaunt to the mall had done one thing. It had calmed my nerves, but now I could feel the tension building again.

"Don't be nervous," Mom told me, but she looked as nervous as I did.

We joined up with Patt, Marc and Mrs. Queen, who had come from the editorial-writing contest. Mrs. Queen was fidgety. She had not one, but three contests to worry about. She looked like she would explode at any minute.

A few minutes before 5, the gray-haired professor emerged from the newsroom. She had the results in her hand. I felt my heart thumping fiercely in my chest.

"I believe I have something you've been waiting for," she said as she tacked the papers on the bulletin board.

The mass of students descended on her, and the professor disappeared from sight. Once again, Mrs. Queen was in the thick of it. I heard a scream from somewhere in the crowd, but this time it wasn't Mrs. Queen. It was someone else.

I nudged my way in to get a closer look. Then, I heard a teacher telling a girl that she won. Someone else had won! I finally pushed through the crowd and got up to the bulletin board where Mrs. Queen was standing.

"You won fourth place!" she said excitedly.

Fourth? My heart sank.

"That's good!" Mrs. Queen said. "That means you're an alternate."

I looked at it another way. I lost. Alternates advanced to the state competition if one of the top three winners couldn't compete, and that wasn't likely. I was disappointed.

Mrs. Queen was trying to tell me I had done well, when the professor appeared again with results of the editorial contest. This was it for Marc and Patt who had been waiting anxiously.

For a brief moment when Marc and Patt were waiting to see their results, I secretly hoped that they wouldn't win. If I couldn't win, I didn't want them to win either. I was selfish. I wanted to keep all the glory for myself.

It was only a brief second, but I hoped they wouldn't get to go to state either. I knew it was wrong of me, and I later asked God to forgive me for harboring selfish feelings toward my classmates.

Neither Patt nor Marc placed in the contest. I felt badly for them afterward. They were my friends. I wanted them to do well, but there was that split second when I let pride and selfishness take control of me.

I was the only one in the group to place. None of the English students who competed the next day placed in their events either. I was the only one.

Everyone was disappointed, but it was a trip none of us would ever forget. Those of us on that trip had a special closeness. We were like family. We celebrated together when we won, and we cried together when we lost.

I learned a valuable lesson about competitiveness. I learned that I didn't have to win to share in someone else's victory. I could be happy for them regardless. Winning or losing doesn't matter. It's what you do with it that counts. I knew God had given me a gift for writing, and I wanted to use it for his purposes.

School let out a few weeks after we returned from regionals, giving way to summer vacation and countless idle hours. I usually welcomed summer break, but I dreaded the year ending.

Writing had taken over my life. I didn't want the year to end. Writing gave me purpose. My life had meaning. As I looked back on that year, I began to see the hand of God directing my life. I didn't know where he was leading me, but I knew I had to trust him to show me his purposes. I knew God had a definite plan for my life. Doubts and fears about the future lingered, but I had a goal, and I'd already started thinking about the fall and my senior year.

The Meaning of Friendship

Everybody took it for granted that I would stay in journalism, but I caught everyone by surprise when I chose my classes my senior year. I enrolled in yearbook instead of staying on the newspaper. Mrs. Queen thought I was making a mistake by not taking the newspaper class, but I thought differently.

Newspapers thrive on deadlines, constant deadlines, and I was afraid of having to meet a deadline every week. Instead, I signed up to work on the yearbook, where deadlines came only once or twice a semester instead of every week.

I had gone back to taking the easy way out instead of facing challenges head-on. I started slacking off again. I'd completed most of the required classes needed to graduate, and I figured I could slide through to graduation.

I padded my schedule with light classes, courses in which I knew I could make an 'A' and protect my class average. I enrolled in a Spanish class of all things. The counselor was aghast when I told him I wanted to take Spanish.

He had a tough enough time deciphering my English. He couldn't imagine why I would take a foreign language, but my friends told me it was an easy class, so I took it.

I often regretted that I slacked off my last year in high school. I lost a year out of my life, a year I could have used to prepare myself for the world that laid just beyond the school doors. I regretted not staying with the newspaper most of all. Working on the newspaper another year would have given me valuable experience, and I let it slip away. It was time that once it was gone, I could never get back.

That year proved helpful to me in other ways. I brought more away from working on the yearbook than I ever expected. And I learned the true meaning of friendship.

Up until then, I had looked at each gesture of kindness offered to me to see whether it was pity or a true offering of friendship. I was skeptical after the mall incident with David.

I was determined to make a place for myself in the harsh world in which I lived, and people saw my perseverance. This became clear to me my senior year in that yearbook class.

It was a small class, with only about 15 writers, but we were more than a class. Patt Richards, besides being editor of the newspaper, was co-editor of the yearbook along with Kambra Winningham.

I delighted over being in class with Kambra again, years after she dashed my boyhood hopes by refusing my plea to be my girlfriend. We had remained friends over the years since we left elementary school and renewed our friendship on the trip to Brownwood.

One Saturday in late October, we had a work day at school. We were approaching our first deadline and had to send a shipment of page proofs to the printer by November or the yearbooks wouldn't arrive by spring.

I wasn't looking forward to spending my Saturday at school. It was the only day I could sleep in, and I could think of plenty other things I'd rather do than go to school. I had a story due for the first deadline, and I'd put off writing it because I thought I had plenty of time. But now the deadline was near and I hadn't even started it.

I stayed up well into the night to finish. Although writing seemed to be a gift, it was never easy. I toiled over every word. I wasn't satisfied until it felt right, and I knew when it wasn't right. I'd write and rewrite it until I had it the way I wanted.

Mom came to my room around midnight to get me to go to bed. "It's late," she said. "You can finish that tomorrow. You don't have to do it all tonight."

I had to finish, though. I couldn't rest until it was done. Mom kept insisting I go to bed so I could get up the next morning, but I kept writing. I had to. I was exhausted, but I had a good feeling knowing I had seen it through.

The next morning, while most of the students drove to school, I rode my three-wheeled bicycle. Mom wanted to drive me, but I insisted on riding. The West Texas north wind was stronger than usual that day. Riding against the wind, the blustery gusts made it difficult to pedal. I kept having to stop to catch my breath. It took me longer to make the eight-block trip that usually took only 10 minutes.

The others were already there when I arrived. I saw their cars parked in front of the school and rushed inside. The building was pitch black. Only an entrance at the other end of the hall let a narrow stream of light escape and guide me down the hall.

It was so quiet it was eerie. I hurried down the darkened hallway to the journalism room.

When I got to the room, there was no one in sight. I didn't think much about it. I figured everyone was in the newsroom, but there were no sounds coming from there either. As I rounded the corner to head into the newsroom, I noticed the lights were out.

I was frightened. I wondered where everyone was when I saw a red streamer hanging from the ceiling. Confused, I proceeded cautiously. Suddenly, lights flooded the room.

"Surprise!" someone yelled. I was caught so off guard that I didn't know what was happening.

"Happy birthday," Mrs. Queen said, as a chorus of others chimed in. My 18th birthday was two days away. I was so stunned I didn't know what to say. "How did you know it was my birthday?" I asked.

Mrs. Queen laughed a cheery titter. "It was all Kambra's idea," she said, giving her a nudge.

"Kambra?"

"I remembered your birthday was in October, and your mom told me the day," Kambra said. Then, they set a work day that day to get me there.

"Are you surprised?" everyone asked.

I never suspected anything like that.

Everyone crowded around me and started singing "Happy Birthday." Then, they brought out a cake. They had it decorated, and it had 18 trick candles.

I took a deep breath and blew as hard as I could, but each time the candles rekindled. I laughed so hard, I cried.

The whole class was in on the surprise, and everyone brought gag gifts. They had things like a fake nose and mustache, which Mrs. Queen ended up wearing before the day was out, and they gave me a birthday card shaped like a yearbook, and everyone had signed it.

It was the best birthday ever. For one day, I was just a normal boy getting together with friends. That day really confirmed in my mind that there were people who didn't pity me. It showed me that I had friends who cared about me. No one had ever done anything like that for me.

I came to see that taking yearbook was the right thing. I often thought I'd made a mistake by leaving the newspaper class, but as the year went on, it became clear that it was the right choice. I cherished the friendships I made in that class. For most of us, it was our last year in high school and the last year we would all be together.

I continued to write, but I started moving in another direction. I turned to editing. It was quite by accident, or maybe God's hand once again, that I started editing.

It was early January, and we were coming upon another deadline and sending another shipment to the printer. The stories had all been edited, and I stayed after school to help get the proofs ready to mail.

Everybody read the stories before they're put on the page, then we read them again. Patt and Kambra made a final check on a story before the pages went in the mail, but even after all those eyes passed over a story, mistakes still slipped by. As I was packing the pages in boxes to mail, I glanced over a story about the cheerleading squad and noticed that the cheerleading sponsor's name was misspelled.

I called Patt's attention to the error, and we were able to change it before we sent in the page. After that, everyone wanted me to proofread their stories. Patt was so grateful I caught the mistake in time that he asked me to be the copy editor. I became a staff member and began to work closely with Patt and Kambra.

My confidence soared. I was thrilled they wanted me to join the staff. I felt like I really had a part in putting out that year's book.

The final deadline was in early March. Everything had to be finished by then to get the book back before school was out in May. With the book finished by March, the only thing left to do was wait.

It was an exciting time of the year. There was such expectation as we moved closer to graduation. There was still much left to do. Classes were still in full swing, and my mind kept wandering as I pondered the fact that I had only a few weeks of high school left.

The long awaited yearbooks arrived the first week of May. There were box loads of them, stacks and stacks of sealed boxes. I'd never seen so many boxes. Everyone, of course, was anxious to look at them, but we had to wait awhile longer.

The particulars about the book were guarded in secrecy. We, on the staff, had been sworn to secrecy all year so as not to divulge any surprises in the book until we unveiled it at an all-school assembly the week before school was out.

It was hard keeping the book a secret when the rest of the school was naturally curious about it and what it looked like. Everybody was asking questions and trying to get a glimpse of it.

We taped newspaper over all the doors and windows in the newsroom to keep onlookers at bay while we sorted the books. We wanted everything to be a surprise.

Finally, the big day arrived. Teachers dismissed classes early for the assembly and a signing party. The school board, principal and all the teachers were present for the unveiling. We painted a larger-than-life, cardboard replica of the cover and shrouded it in linens until the appropriate time.

Then, with everyone assembled in the fieldhouse and all eyes fixed on the giant piece of cardboard, Patt lowered the veil to reveal the 1987 Harvester yearbook. The crowd gasped in approval.

It was a simple design, a basic gray background with green stripes diagonally across the cover. In the center was a bubble-shaped quotation and the words "You said it . . .," the theme for the year. The book was filled with hundreds of quotes from students and teachers. It was their book, so we quoted as many people as we could on everything from football to fashion.

A rousing round of cheers and shouts rose as the audience expressed its pleasure with the cover.

Patt also made special presentations during the assembly. Those of us in yearbook knew he was going to present copies of the annual to the school board members and to four retiring teachers. But I was not prepared for what happened next. After Patt presented the four teachers their copies of the yearbook he sat down, and Kambra stepped to the platform.

She began by saying the yearbook staff had a special person they wanted to dedicate the book to. I was kind of confused because we hadn't talked about dedicating the book to anyone. I didn't occur to me who she was talking about until she said it was a person who worked on the yearbook and is "one member of our family whose determination is admired by all."

Then, I realized she was talking about me. I sat there in disbelief. Kambra said it was a person "whose courage and friendship we admire and cherish. The yearbook staff wishes to dedicate this year's book to our friend Chris Ely."

I was motionless. I didn't know what to do. Mrs. Queen started waving wildly for me to come up on the stage. I stood up, my legs trembling, and started toward the platform as the audience stood and applauded.

I felt tears coming to my eyes as I made my way to the stage. It seemed to take me a lifetime to walk from where I was seated on the bottom row of the bleachers up to the stage. When I reached the platform, I could think of nothing else to do but lean over and hug Kambra as she handed me a copy of the yearbook. It was the happiest moment of my life.

After I returned to my seat, I got another surprise. Kambra called Mom from the audience and presented her with a copy of the annual. I didn't know that Mom was in the audience. I learned later that they called Mom and told her something special was going to happen at the assembly. She wasn't told what was going to happen, only that she needed to be there.

It was an emotional afternoon. Friends and classmates and some I didn't even know came to me after the assembly and said they admired me. When the crowd had cleared, I choked back tears as I read the words the staff penned to me on a dedication page in the back of the book.

I cherished their words and the love in them. It meant that my efforts were not in vain. People really did understand me. Whether I realized it or not, people were watching me. Not because I was different, but because my determination made them want more for themselves.

Graduation Day

The days leading to graduation were full of emotion as I prepared to leave Pampa High and say good-bye to friends I'd known since grade school. Friends who had drifted away over the years and I'd not talked to in a while came back for a final farewell.

I had a special reunion with my old grade-school friend Derrick Smith. He watched out for me, picked me up when I fell, or else told me to get up; he protected me. But over the years as we grew and changed and our interests grew apart, we began to drift apart.

The night of our graduation, we rekindled our friendship. I had my gown on, and we were lining up for the procession. I was trying desperately to keep that flat-top, cardboard cap from sliding off my head when Derrick came over.

"This is it," he said, solemnly.

"I know. Are you ready?" I asked.

"I don't think so."

"Me either."

"I want you to know I'm proud of you, and what you've done. I'll never forget you, you know."

"I'll never forget what you've done for me," I said.

Derrick stretched out his arms to hug me. I tried to force back tears as we embraced warmly. Emotions were running high that night. A melancholy feeling hovered in the halls. I soon would depart those hallowed halls. I was excited about graduating, but the uncertainty of the future left me with mixed emotions.

I was unsure what would happen in the weeks and months to follow. I had made no decisions about the future beyond graduation, but I trusted that God would provide.

That night promised the unexpected. Ominous, dark clouds hung overhead, bringing the threat of rain. Everyone hoped the storm would hold off until after the ceremony. The procession led us outside the main building where the line formed to the fieldhouse for the ceremony.

I stood to the side as the class began lining up. My body was more tense than ever, and my coordination was as poor as it had ever been. I knew I wouldn't be able to keep pace with the beat of the march, and I didn't want to slow the class down, so the teachers arranged for me to slip in and take my place just before the march began.

I was all ready to go in when the senior class sponsor stopped me. He instructed me to line up with the class. I tried telling him I wasn't marching in the procession, but he said there had been a change of plans.

Some students had gone to him before the ceremony and told him they wanted me to march with the class. They didn't care if I couldn't keep up or if I slowed down the line. I was part of the class, and I should march in. I was thrilled that they wanted to include me. It meant a lot to me that they wanted to include me.

The students cheered as I took my place in line. My heart was pounding fiercely as the music started. This was it, the minute I'd dreamed about.

They divided us into two groups. Half the class entered the fieldhouse from the east side; the other half from the west. The groups marched down the outside aisles, crossed the back of the room and came up the center aisle together.

Instead of going all the way around, they told me I could march until I came even with my row, then cut across and take my seat. It was still like marching with the class, but I wouldn't hold up the line.

The music began, and the line started in. I advanced a couple of feet when I noticed the gap between me and the students ahead of me starting to widen. I couldn't keep the pace of the march. I was falling behind. I walked slowly and cautiously so I wouldn't lose my balance. I felt like every eye in the room was trained on me.

I only had to make it to the first row, then I would drop out of line and take my seat. It couldn't have been more than 10 or 15 feet, but it seemed much farther. I kept a steady pace toward my goal. I came to my row and darted in. I was in the last seat on the first row.

I remember little about the speeches or the ceremony that evening. Kambra was class valedictorian. As she stood up before the class to deliver the farewell address and speak of the future, I couldn't help remembering the past and the times we had shared together.

Kambra always had been the class leader. I felt proud knowing my friend was up there delivering the valedictory speech. I cherished the friendship we had. I never knew for sure, but I always believed Kambra was responsible for me marching with the class. I was deeply touched by her gestures of friendship.

I was terrified at the mere thought of crossing the stage in front of all those people. My whole family — Mom, Dad, grandparents, aunts, uncles and cousins — turned out to see me graduate.

The honor students went forward first to receive their diplomas. I was on the tail end of the top 10 percent of the class. The principal called the names of the honor students in the order of class rank.

One by one, students crossed the stage to receive their diplomas. I waited for him to call my name.

Finally, I heard my name.

I stepped onto the platform, my legs shaking violently. I was petrified. Midway across the stage, I took the diploma in my left hand and shook the principal's hand with my right. Suddenly, the entire class stood and erupted in applause, as the audience joined in a standing ovation.

The applause lingered as I left the stage and returned to my seat with the class. I cannot describe my feelings as I sat there, half oblivious to my surroundings, and watched my friends pass across the stage to receive their diplomas. We finally made it. We had graduated.

The thunderstorm had moved overhead as the ceremony ended and we left the fieldhouse, ready to begin a new chapter in our lives. It was sort of a sign of what lay ahead. There would be storms to weather along the way, but with hard work and perseverance we'd weather the storms.

I cherished my memories of high school and my years in school. It was one of the most carefree and happiest times of my life, and I knew my life would never be the same again.

Leap of Faith

❧

I always believed if I worked hard and trusted in God, I
could move mountains — even if I had to trudge a few
valleys along the way. It was only through faith in God that
I was able to do anything. He helped me in the good times
and carried me through the hard times.

After high school, all my attention turned to college. I
had given much thought to the future. I knew my calling
was to be a journalist. The only question now was how to
turn my dream into a reality. Summer was quickly approaching, and I still had many unsettled questions, wondering if
I would go to college in the fall or if I could get a job once
I finished. Still, I had to believe God had a plan for my life.

Mom and Dad never really talked about college with me.
Why get my hopes up over something that might never happen, they asked themselves. Although they hoped there would
be something I could do after high school, they had doubts
about sending me away to college. They didn't feel I was capable of going away to school. They braced for the worse:
that I might never be able to live on my own. They only wanted
the best for their son, but the odds seemed too great.

Whenever I mentioned college, my parents said, "We'll have to wait and see." But now, it was time for me to make decisions. I had to make my future happen.

I was determined that things would be different after high school. No longer was I content to sit around and do nothing. I had to find a job.

Mrs. Queen graciously offered her help in the job search. As soon as school was out, she called her friend at the newspaper, hoping he would let me work there for the summer.

I was willing to do any job at the paper, even if it meant taking no pay at first. I just wanted someone to give me a chance.

Weeks passed, and I heard nothing from the newspaper. I was beginning to lose all hope when I received a reply. The editor gently but resolutely turned me down. Without experience or a college degree, there was nothing he could do.

No one would give me a chance. I decided the only chance I had of getting a job was to go to college and get a degree.

I carefully devised a plan to convince my parents I was ready for college. I had it all worked out. I could go to school with Bill, I thought. We could be roommates, and he could help me.

Bill and I always vowed we would go to college together. Bill's mom once joked if we were roommates Bill could cook and help me, and I could help him with his studies. She was joking, but it was no joke to me. I saw Bill as my only chance to go away to school in the fall.

My dream was shattered when things didn't work out as I planned. Bill decided not to go to college. He'd had enough school and wanted to work after graduation. Then, there was my parents. They always assumed I would enroll at the community college and live at home.

I was heartbroken, of course. I had my heart set on going away to school. But for now anyway I would have to be content going to a junior college and living with my parents. It wouldn't be that bad, I assured myself, and it would just be for a couple of years. I could take some classes, then in a couple of years transfer to a four-year school. I always kept that dream alive in my heart — that I would go away to college.

When school started in the fall, Dad took me to enroll at Clarendon College-Pampa Center. The picture I had of seeing the campus for the first time is etched in my mind. There was a meager one building, an old elementary school that the college leased and turned into a makeshift campus. It was the stepchild of Clarendon College's main campus 50 miles away, which had lush dormitories and a modern library.

Clarendon College opened a Pampa campus to attract the growing number of students returning to college after a great oil depression in the late '70s. Temporary classrooms were set up in the high school basement until a permanent place was found in the abandoned grade school. The building was old and dilapidated. Hardly what I imagined college would be like.

The desks sat only a few feet off the ground. Most of the school's enrollment was older, making it a tight fit for some to squeeze into the tiny chairs that seemed more suited to grade schoolers than college freshmen.

Drinking fountains and bathroom sinks were lower, too. At first, I thought they were lower to accommodate people in wheelchairs. I always looked to see if buildings were accessible, and this one certainly was even if their purpose had been to accommodate smaller students rather than disabled people.

I started off slowly with only three classes the first semester. I had to prove — mostly to myself — that I could handle the rigorous college work. I didn't know what to expect.

It wasn't much different from high school. A sea of familiar faces greeted me on the first day of class. I thought I was the only one stuck living at home going to a junior college. I was surprised when I saw friends from high school turn up there, too. Turns out, I wasn't the only one.

The students weren't the only reminders of high school. The college recruited its core of small, but dedicated faculty from the public schools, allowing instructors to teach at the college at night. I had the same algebra teacher that I had in high school.

Mixed in among the fresh-faced high school graduates was a group of older students returning to school to get their degrees. I found acceptance among the older students that I didn't have with people my age. They accepted me, while the younger ones still considered me an outsider.

The older crowd welcomed me into their study sessions and invited me for coffee after class. They treated me like a guest instead of an intruder. I made many lasting friendships.

I was fond of one woman in particular. Reba was old enough to be my mother. She hadn't been inside a classroom in 20 years, but she was following her heart. She wanted to get her degree. Being older, she knew it would be hard, but she set a goal and went after it.

She struggled to keep up with the younger, sprier students. We learned to help each other. We studied together after class, and she gave me rides home because I did not have a car.

Although Reba was older, I was more at ease with her than with those my own age. We had something in common. We were both following our dreams. College came at a price for both of us. We had to work harder to reach our goals.

The older students inspired me. I saw them and thought if they could do it, surely I could make it in college.

After taking a lighter load the first year to reassure myself I could handle college work, I was ready for a greater challenge. I took a full load my second year at Clarendon: 15 hours. The classes were more advanced now, and I had to buckle down and study. Chemistry was the hardest, and it taught me quite a lesson about life.

A retired Baptist minister taught the class. He had taught biology and chemistry at the high school for years before retiring. He came out of retirement to teach this one class at the college two nights a week. Just my luck.

I put off taking any science classes until my second year, and chemistry was the only science course offered that semester. The class centered around a lab. One night a week was strictly lab work, which counted for half our grade. I was nervous because I knew I'd have trouble working with chemicals for the experiments.

I talked to the instructor, who was getting up in years. He assured me the lab work wouldn't be a problem. "Don't worry about it. I'll help you," he said in his deep preaching voice. I could do what I could in the lab and observe the experiments I couldn't do.

My mind was put at ease after talking to the instructor. I went into the class confident that he would work with me and not penalize me because of my physical limitations. After all, I had never had a problem before with a teacher modifying my assignments when I needed help.

I had no trouble with the written assignments. I picked up the concepts right away. When we started labs a few weeks into the semester, I was matched up with a lab partner.

The old instructor paired me with his most advanced student. My partner was well-versed in the sciences. He worked in a chemical plant. He only took the class because he needed it to get a degree.

Some experiments required only simple operations, and I performed these tasks with no trouble. When it came time for complex experiments that involved mixing chemicals, I merely watched while my partner did the hands-on work.

My lab partner was very patient and kind. I never was that fond of science, so his experience was helpful in explaining the experiment as we went along. I was able to grasp the concepts behind the experiment without actually performing the hands-on work.

As the semester progressed, I was doing well in the class, or so I thought. I made A's on all the tests and my homework. It came as a surprise when the semester ended and I got my grade in the mail. I got a 'B' in the class, the only 'B' that I had made since I started college. I couldn't understand it because I had made A's on everything all year.

The grade confounded me. I thought maybe I failed the final exam. I studied. I couldn't understand it, so I called the instructor. He said it wasn't that I hadn't done well on the test. He said he couldn't give me an 'A' because I hadn't done the labs.

I was angry. It wasn't fair. I had done the work. I felt like telling him I had worked every bit as hard as everyone else in the class, maybe more so. I needed help from time to time, but in the end I did the work and I got the same results as everyone else.

The instructor further advised me that I shouldn't take any advanced chemistry courses. It infuriated me that he would tell me not to take a class, not that I would have considered taking another class from him. It was just unfair that he would penalize me for something beyond my control. I could have understood it if I hadn't done the work, but I had.

Life isn't always fair. There are going to be battles. I could have fought the grade, but sometimes you have to accept that life isn't always fair and forge ahead.

By that time, I had taken all the classes I could take at Clarendon College, and after two years I began to think in earnest again about going away to school.

I knew that if it was going to happen, I was going to have to make it happen. I had taken all the classes I could take at the Pampa Center, and now I had to make a decision. I started talking to Mom and Dad about going to the university. They were skeptical, but they agreed to let me try.

That spring, I sent letters to colleges in the area. I wrote to West Texas State University and Texas Tech University. I first had to find out if the campuses were accessible or if they lagged behind like the high school, which didn't even have an elevator until my junior year. With a three-wheel bike as my only means of transportation, I had to find a place where I could get around easily by foot or bicycle.

I received little response from either school. I got a standard reply: a copy of the college catalog and an application for admission, but nothing about accessibility.

The chances of me getting to go to college were looking slim. By the middle of July, I still hadn't found out anything. It was beginning to look like I wasn't going to college that fall.

I didn't give up. I begged my parents to take me to West Texas State University to talk to the coordinator for disabled students. So, three weeks before school was to start, Mom, Dad and I went to WT.

Our first stop was the admissions office. The admissions' director showed us the campus. I was surprised that most buildings were accessible. There were elevators and ramps in almost every building.

As we toured the campus, Mom was still skeptical. "It's so big. How would you ever get around?" she asked.

I had a different view of campus. It wasn't that big; it was really quite compact. I could picture myself on campus, jetting from building to building on my bicycle easily. I was more determined than ever to go to school there.

The campus was deserted on that sweltering, summer day. It was between semesters, and most of the students and faculty had left for a two-week break before the fall term began. We went to the disabled student services office and the journalism department, only to find that the people we needed to see were off campus that day. I filled out scholarship applications and left copies of my transcript.

I left WT knowing little more than I did when I got there. It was beginning to look like I was going to have to sit out that semester, and my dream of getting my degree would remain just that — a dream. All I could do now was pray for a miracle between then and the time school started.

The Master's Plan

A miracle did happen. The next day, the head of the school's communications department called. He had received my transcript. He offered me a journalism scholarship. My hopes soared. I still had a chance.

Now, I really had to make a decision. Until then, it was all just talk. Now, I had to decide. I didn't know if I could make it on my own. I asked Dad if he thought I could make it away from home.

"That's something you're going to have to decide for yourself," he said. "Only you know if you can do it." Even though they still had doubts, my parents would support me whatever I decided to do.

I didn't know, but one thing was certain. I had to try. If I didn't try, I would never know.

There was still much to work out before school started, whether I should get a roommate and live in the dorm, what classes to take, how I would get to class in bad weather. I believed if it was God's will, he would provide a way.

Mom worried about everything. Although she was proud of my accomplishments, she worried I was fooling myself by thinking I could be something I couldn't. She was afraid I was setting myself up for a let down. She wanted to spare me some of the hurts of reality. Mom was looking at reality. In the natural, I couldn't do what I was setting out to do. But I saw through the eyes of faith.

Still in doubt, Mom called the dean at West Texas to see if we could meet with the journalism professors to discuss my chances of becoming a journalist. That's when everything fell into place. It was as if God had gone ahead of me to clear the way.

The head of the communications department, Dr. Robert Vartabedian, was helpful beyond belief. He had everything ready when we arrived at his office. He told us about the scholarship and the journalism program, and he arranged for me to meet with the two journalism instructors.

Rick Carpenter was the student adviser, and Nancy Hansen was a journalism instructor. Neither fit the image I had of college professors. I had pictured professors as old, gray-haired men. Rick was a tall, slender man. He was very astute and businesslike that day. Nancy was young as well. She was very friendly and energetic.

Mom had told them about my cerebral palsy when she talked to them on the phone. They seemed almost as surprised when they saw me as I was about them. They watched as I shuffled across the room to greet them.

The instructors were very willing to talk to Mom and me. They told me about the journalism program and what classes I should take the first semester.

But they were honest in telling me that with my speech difficulties, I'd have a tough time making it as a reporter.

But I persisted. They enrolled me in a beginning journalism class and suggested I write articles for the yearbook. While the instructors advised me on classes, Dr. Vartabedian called the coordinator for disabled students and the campus housing director. They were waiting for us when we finished scheduling my classes. The housing director took us to show us the dorms. I debated whether I should get a roommate or ask for a private room. It would be nice having someone to help me, but a roommate might think I was a burden. Maybe no one would want to room with me, I thought. I was torn over what to do.

The dorm director described two rooms to us. Both were accessible for disabled students. He would show us both, and I could decide which one I liked.

The first room was in a seven-story dormitory. As we walked up the sidewalk to the building, I looked skyward at the massive structure. I could hardly believe I was standing there and might actually be living there. My heart was racing with excitement.

The director took us inside and down a long hallway to a room at the end of the hall. The room was much larger than I expected. It had been refurbished to make it more accessible. One of the desks was lower so someone in a wheelchair could roll up to it easily, and one bed had an electric lift. Even the doors had push levers instead of door knobs. I was beaming with glee. It was exactly what I needed.

Mom still had some questions before she could give her blessing. "What about the bathroom?" she asked. That was where I would need the most help. At home, Dad put a handrail on the side of the bathtub for support, so I could pull myself up out of the tub.

As the dorm director led us down the hall to the bathroom, I expected to see a wall of showers instead of a bathtub. Most dormitories had only showers. I never took showers. The slick, wet surface made it impossible for me to keep my balance. I was afraid of slipping. I didn't know how I would manage if there was no tub.

I could hardly believe it when I walked into the restroom. There was a regular shower next to the door, and back in the corner was a bathtub — complete with handrails like the ones at home.

It was hard to believe the way everything worked out that day. It was as if that room was meant for me. The housing director even offered to let me have the room as a private room. I wouldn't have to worry about finding someone who would want to share a room with me.

We didn't look at the other room. I didn't need to see any others. I knew that room was meant for me. It had to be.

As we left the school that day, I told Mom it was no coincidence the way things had worked out. It had to be God. There was no other explanation for the way things fell into place that day. Mom agreed that it was as if I was meant to be there. She felt better about me going away then. After seeing the obstacles being rolled away, Mom knew she couldn't stand in my way. She had to let me go.

College Bound

The day I left for college was the day I saw my dream become a reality. I waited two long years for that day, and it wasn't until the car was packed and we were on the way that I realized my dream of going to college was coming true. I was on my way to independence.

It was harder on Mom than it was on me, knowing she would have to leave me at the end of the day. Mom had stood by me and supported me through it all. It was hard for her to let me go, but she stood by me. Dad too.

They knew how much it meant to me, and they supported me. They kept silent even though they still had doubts. Sink or swim, I'd have to stand on my own now. They knew I'd take some falls, but they encouraged me and let me stand on my own.

Finally, the time we had both dreaded had arrived. It was time to say good-bye. Choking back tears, we said our good-byes. I hugged Mom and told her I would be all right, then I watched as she slowly drove away.

A strange feeling came over me as I watched Mom pull away. It wasn't a sad feeling, but I wasn't as excited as I thought I would be. For a minute, I wanted to run after her, yelling, "Stop! Don't leave me here!" But then, I realized this was what I had wanted for so long. The future stood before me. I only had to look to God to know I was going to be all right.

Mom got a few blocks from the school and had to pull off the road. She had put up a tough front while she was with me, but now tears began to caress her face. She had a good cry before she started home.

Slowly, I made my way back into the dormitory filled with strangers. I wondered if they would accept me and give me a chance. It really didn't sink in on me that I was finally on my own. That thought frightened me.

That night, there was a cookout on the lawn outside the cafeteria. Tables were spread out beneath the trees, and some students were sprawled on the ground feasting on hamburgers and ice cream. I was at a loss as to what to do. I couldn't eat on the ground, but how could I carry my plate to the table without dropping it?

My hands quaked violently at the thought of trying to steady the tray and carry the food without spilling it. I didn't dare ask for help. What would people think? I was on my own now. I couldn't ask for help. I took a tray and got in line.

When I reached the front of the line, the lady serving noticed I was having trouble balancing the tray. She quickly summoned one of the cafeteria workers to come carry my food. The tables were full by the time I got through the line. I sat down on the cafeteria steps well away from the crowd, hoping no one would notice if I dripped lemonade down my shirt.

I watched the other students as they milled around, laughing and greeting friends they hadn't seen all summer. They all looked so happy. How I wanted to rush over and join them, but I kept my distance for now. A group of freshmen came over after recognizing me from moving into the dorm earlier that day. Their warm greeting was a welcome surprise.

"You live in Jones Hall, don't you?" one of the boys asked.

"Yes," I said surprised they had recognized me.

"We live on the seventh floor. You'll have to come up."

"Thanks," I said, thinking they were just being friendly and that they didn't really want my company. I simply couldn't believe they meant it. They were just being kind, I told myself.

I quickly finished my burger and left. I had refused any ice cream, afraid it would get soft and run down my chin. It had been a long day, and I was exhausted.

That night, the excitement began to sit in. I could hardly sleep. I lay in bed listening intently to the unfamiliar voices on the floor above me. There was never a quiet moment in the dorm. The noise didn't bother me. I was just thrilled to actually be there. I fell asleep, assuring myself everything would be all right.

The next day was the only free day before classes began. I spent the day riding around looking at the campus. I was all wide-eyed as I explored my new surroundings on my three-wheel bicycle.

I found the building where my classes met. The fine arts building was as far on the other side of campus from my room as you could get. Still, it took me only about 10 minutes by bike. I remembered Mom's warning when we first visited the school and how hard she said it would be to get around in such a big place. Suddenly, it didn't seem as big or as scary.

I rode around admiring the beautiful, old buildings that had been restored and renovated. They were beautiful. The lawns were green and meticulously groomed.

I was riding back to my room when a girl rode up beside me on a bicycle. She was looking at me rather curiously so I stopped, thinking she wanted to get around me.

She was friendly and smiled warmly. "I was just admiring your bike," she said as she rode up beside me.

"Thanks," I said. "I'm glad to see someone else on a bike." My three-wheeler stuck out among all the other people walking, and I felt a little out of place anyway.

She asked my name and said we should go riding together sometime. We talked awhile before I went back to the dorm. It was nice to see a friendly face in a place that seemed so foreign. Still, I had to question whether her gesture was sincere or if she was just being polite.

Classes got under way the next day. I had only one class the first day. It was an 8 o'clock class, and without Mom there to prod me, I had to get up and get dressed by myself. I was up early because it took me longer to get ready, struggling to get my socks and shoes on, which was still difficult for me. At last, I was on my way to class.

I saw Dr. Vartabedian on my way to class. He was one of the few people whose kindness I accepted as a genuine willingness to help me. I thought everyone else was just doing it for show. Dr. Vartabedian showed me a safe place to stow my bike and walked me to the elevator.

The elevator was tucked away in the back of the building. I might have never known it was there if he hadn't pointed it out. Music students used it to cart their instruments to a second-floor music room. I actually had to pass through the music room to reach the elevator. I wasted more steps walking to the elevator than I saved by riding it, so I took the stairs after that.

My first class was public relations, and we lost little time before we started writing. We got an assignment the first day. Nancy Hansen, one of the instructors I had met a week earlier in Dr. Vartabedian's office, divided the class in groups of two. We had to interview our partner and write a profile of the other person.

The class was one shy of everyone having a partner and by the time the instructor got to me, everyone already had a match. Everyone was already starting to shuffle their chairs and beginning to interview someone.

There was a woman there named Lydia who came to class with a hearing-impaired student. She was an interpreter for the student who read lips.

I interviewed Lydia. She went around to classes with the hearing-impaired student and translated the instructor's lectures using sign language. I was comforted knowing there were other disabled students on campus. I wasn't alone in the battle for independence. There were others like me.

Taste of Independence

Gradually, I settled in and began to make adjustments trying to survive on my own. I rode my bike everywhere. I never could have made it across the campus without my three-wheeler. It was like having an extra pair of legs.

One morning, I got up and it was raining. It was a cold, driving rain. It fell in sheets and pounded the ground. I knew I'd get soaked if I tried to ride to class.

I waited a few minutes, praying the rain would let up. It came down in droves. I knew it was no use to try to ride my bike that day, but I had to get to class. I walked down to the lobby hoping someone with a car would see me and offer me a ride. I was ready to give up when I spotted Tim, the resident assistant on my floor.

Resident assistants were upperclassmen who lived in the dorm and helped the residents adjust to college life. I was determined not to ask anyone for help, but I could see no other way. I had to get to class. I got up the nerve and asked for a ride.

Tim was headed the other direction, but he offered to drop me at the fine arts building on the way. I was never so grateful for a ride. I didn't want to miss class, especially because of a little rain. Winter would be coming on soon, and I didn't know what I was going to do then. I just took it one day at a time and trusted in God to help me.

The thing I dreaded most was mealtime and eating among strangers. I went to the cafeteria at odd hours after most students had left. I waited until midafternoon or late at night to avoid crowds.

Every other Thursday night was steak night at the cafeteria. It was a rare treat, when the fare was a little better than the usual choice of turkey fritters and soy patties.

I went to the cafeteria that first Thursday thinking I would enjoy some good home cooking, but what I got instead was a taste of humility.

We had a choice of chopped sirloin or chicken-fried steak. I chose chicken-fried, thinking it would be easier to manage. Mom always cut up my meat for me, but I thought I'd be able to manage. It looked tender, and I was sure I could manage a little piece of steak.

I took the knife and tried to slice off a small piece. The steak was smothered in gravy and when I tried to cut it, the gravy ran off but the knife didn't cut through the meat. I tried to cut another piece, but my knife kept slipping. The steak slid off the plate and almost went in my lap. I recovered it before it landed on the floor. The knife had scraped all the crust off but wouldn't cut the meat.

Finally, I gave up. In frustration, I picked up the whole piece of steak with my fingers and started to bite into it when I noticed a girl watching me from the balcony. I froze. She must have been watching me the whole time. She got up and started toward my table. I wanted to crawl under the table or disappear.

I was embarrassed. The girl asked if she could cut my steak for me. I was grateful but humiliated. I was supposed to be doing it on my own. I couldn't enjoy the rest of my meal.

That night, I started to have second thoughts about whether I could make it at college. I went back to my room and started questioning whether I'd made the right decision. If I couldn't cut a piece of steak, how could I manage other tasks? I began to pray, "God, you brought me this far. Don't leave me now." I knew I couldn't make it without God. He was my strength, especially in those first few weeks at college.

As much as I relied on my parents to do everything for me when I was young, now I was determined to make it on my own. All on my own. I had to find that balance between independence and being dependent on others.

I realized it was all right to admit I needed help. I couldn't do it all by myself. I was going to need some help. After that, I wasn't afraid to ask for help when I needed it.

One kind cafeteria worker graciously carried my tray and cut up my meat and anything else I needed. Billy Rowe helped me with my food every day. He'd see me come in and rush out to help me.

Billy was a patient, gentle man. He waited while I tried to decide what I wanted to eat and then made sure I didn't need anything else cut or poured before he went back to his post in the dish room. After a week or two, he knew what to cut up without me telling him.

Billy was a man of strong conviction. He did a lot to encourage me in my faith. At a time when I was torn between living a fast and loose college life or following the Christian scruples my parents so sternly instilled in me, Billy was like a spiritual beacon.

Away from home for the first time, it was easy to forsake the principles of godly living and follow the crowd. Mom wasn't there to prod me to get out of bed on Sunday morning and go to church. I could have easily stayed in bed an extra hour, especially since I had no way of getting to church. But then there was Billy.

He graciously offered to take me to church services with him. I gladly accepted his invitation, if for no other reason than just to be with someone. The halls were always swarming with people, but I often felt like I was on an island isolated from everybody.

I loved going to church with Billy. He was raised much as I was in a Pentecostal Assembly of God church. The church had a lot of older saints, fervent prayer warriors. I went through many falls my first year away from home. Their prayers lifted my faith. It gave me hope when I felt like giving up.

After church, Billy sometimes invited me to his home for Sunday dinner. I delighted in any chance at a home-cooked meal away from the school cafeteria, and Billy always remembered to cut up my food. At times, I think he thought I was helpless. He insisted on helping me into the car and buckling my seat belt. I needed help with my food, so he assumed I couldn't do anything for myself. I had to remind him, "I can do it. I'm not helpless."

Billy was a friend at a time when I was alone and needed an ally. The loneliness was suffocating the first few months I was there. Mom and Dad told me it would be hard at first, but they assured me I'd make friends. It wasn't that easy for me. I couldn't talk to strangers.

I was determined that I was going to be more open in college than in high school. Things would be different at college, I told myself. I would go up and talk to people and let them get to know me. I would be one of the boys, and they would want to be with me.

I tried to open up and talk to the guys in the dorm. I tried to fit in, but it was the same as high school. I was still an outsider. The guys in the dorm were friendly, but that's as far as it went. The fact was I didn't fit in. There was a barrier that wouldn't crumble. No matter how hard I tried, I could never be one of the boys.

I joined the handicapped student-support group on campus, where I made friends with other disabled students. I saw what they went through, their struggles, their trials and I realized I wasn't alone. I was no different from any other student there. Everyone struggled, and we learned to help each other.

Rusty Tomlinson was the disabled students coordinator. He helped us work to reach our goals. Rusty was a graduate student. He wanted to help disabled children when he finished school.

He called me nearly every day; he often took me to lunch and encouraged me to keep trying. And when I turned 21, he bought me my first beer. I only took a few swigs. It tasted bitter and made me sick to my stomach. I swore I'd never drink again. I knew it was wrong to drink, but it was a rite of passage, and I had to try it.

Trials and Testing

Fall rolled into winter, and the frigid weather kept me inside more. My classes were mostly in the morning, and I had the rest of the day idle. I stayed in my room, mostly by myself. I was lonely. Mom called nearly every day. I looked forward to her calls and the sound of another voice, and I wanted to go home every weekend.

I begged my parents to come get me on weekends. Dad made the 75-mile trip to pick me up on Friday, and he took me back Sunday afternoon. I didn't want to stay at school on weekends. When the weather was too bad and I had to stay on campus, I locked myself in my room. It got so bad that at one point, I said if I made it through the semester, I didn't want to go back.

The only thing that kept me from giving up was my classes. I was finally doing what I loved. I took only journalism classes the first semester. I hadn't written anything since high school. It had been two years, and I had missed writing. I was nervous about writing again, but it all came back the first time I sat down at the typewriter.

There wasn't much writing at first. I had to start at the bottom. My classes were filled with mostly freshmen. I was almost a junior and eager to write again.

I knew there would be plenty of chances to write later on, but I didn't want to wait. I had all these ideas in my head, and writing was the only way I knew to get them out. I expressed my desire to write to Rick Carpenter. He echoed my fears from high school that the deadlines of a weekly newspaper might be too much for me, and he suggested I write for the yearbook.

Rick took an interest in me and warmly welcomed me into the yearbook class. Still, he couldn't help but wonder if I could meet the stiff demands made on reporters. He watched with growing concern the difficulty I had communicating. He was hesitant to send me out on interviews, so he gave me a special assignment: to write articles for a newsmagazine section in the yearbook.

The yearbook editor gave me a stack of Newsweek and Time magazines. I read about the events in the magazines and wrote an account of what I read. It was a historic year. There was plenty of material. The Berlin Wall came crashing down that fall, and Hurricane Hugo left a path of destruction as it swept across the East Coast.

I didn't have to worry about interviews and the frustrations of not being understood, and I liked writing news articles. I worked on the stories for two solid weeks, writing and rewriting, painstakingly choosing each word. Finally, I turned my first story in to the editor.

My heart was bursting with excitement as I handed her my story. I watched as she skimmed the pages I had pounded out on my old typewriter. I was beaming with pride, only to have her hand back my story and ask me if I had copied it from the magazine.

Later that afternoon in my adviser's office, Rick explained to me about plagiarism and how it was wrong — not to mention illegal — to take the words of others and pass them off as your own.

I didn't understand. I sweated over those words for two weeks, carefully choosing each one. It was my work. I wrote those articles. I handed Rick the magazines and told him to see for himself.

That night, I cried myself to sleep. No one believed I was capable of writing that article. More than ever, I vowed that I would not return to school in the spring. How could I if no one believed in me?

I was angry. I cried out to God. Why would he bring me this far to watch me fail? But I didn't give up. I continued to trust God. I knew he would see me through.

When I went back to class the next week, Rick returned the magazines. He had compared the magazine articles to my work, and he saw that he was wrong. He told me I was blessed with a special talent. Rick gave me back the magazines and asked me to keep writing the articles.

I persevered and finished the semester, but it wasn't without much help and encouragement from my professors. Although the first few months at college were lonely, I wondered what I'd do with my life if I didn't go back. I knew my only hope of finding a job was a college degree. I had to try.

The second semester brought less trials than the first. Gradually, I relaxed and adjusted to being on my own. I accepted being alone, and I found that the way to forget about the loneliness was to get involved. I threw myself into my studies. I took another writing class and started writing for the college newspaper.

It was different from the articles I wrote from magazines. I actually had to talk to people. I was afraid they would reject me. It created a problem getting stories, but the professors were understanding. They worked with me to help me get interviews. Each week, either Rick or Nancy would call and set up the interview, then I'd go and talk to them in person.

I had no trouble when I went to talk to them in person even though I had a rather crude technique for interviewing. I wrote down my questions and gave them a copy. It was less awkward that way. They didn't feel embarrassed when they didn't understand me, and I didn't get as frustrated if they couldn't comprehend right away.

I submitted an article each week, hoping each time my story would get in the paper. It was weeks before I got a story in the paper, but I was so proud when I finally got my first story printed.

The story was on faith. I wrote about the campus minister at the Methodist Student Center and his mission in helping students explore their faith. College is a time for searching, and as a minister, he helped students deal with life's uncertainties — not to provide all the answers, but to help them discover their own beliefs.

I learned something from writing that story because I was at that stage of searching, and I thought other students could learn, too. I submitted the story, not knowing if it would get in the paper, and the editor liked it. She printed it that week.

More than anything, though, the editors were surprised by my writing. People thought someone "with my condition" was incapable of accomplishing a goal like going to college or writing a story. "He shouldn't be able to do that," they said.

I had to dispel the stereotypes people had about me and other disabled individuals and, in time, people began to look past the physical defects and see my abilities.

The editors began to see that I was capable of doing the work. Over the semester, they began to assign me more difficult subjects to write about. I received choice assignments.

In time, Rick also began to believe in me. He believed I had a gift, and he unselfishly devoted time to help me.

Shortly before the semester ended, Rick arranged an interview with the *Amarillo Globe-News* for a summer internship. The job was for a copy editor. Writing was my first love, but Rick convinced me I'd have a better chance landing a job as a copy editor than as a reporter. I was ready to try anything at that point.

I went to the newspaper for an interview and an intense editing test. I hadn't done much editing since high school. The test didn't go well. I panicked when they handed me a story and told me to edit it. I sat staring down at the paper. I didn't even finish the test. Needless to say, I didn't get the internship.

I was heartbroken, and Rick was almost as disappointed as I was. He really wanted me to do well. Rick encouraged me not to give up. I was, after all, still a junior. I had time.

I was discouraged when I left school for the summer. Despite some success with my writing, I still had been unable to get a job. I had prayed I would get that internship so I could work that summer. I didn't want to spend another summer at home. But it wasn't meant to be.

A Second Chance

After the fiasco of the editing test, I wanted to give up. I felt like I had failed. I had to be the only person who had ever been turned down for a job, I thought. I sulked for weeks. Again, I vowed I would not return to school in the fall.

I had been home only a few weeks and already was getting restless from the dog days of summer when I got a call from Renita Finney. Renita was the new editor of the college newspaper, and she offered me a job as copy editor for the fall semester.

Of course, I was thrilled. I knew it was only because of Rick that she even considered me for the job, but I was glad to accept. This was my chance to prove to Mom and Dad that I could make it as a journalist.

The promise of a job gave me new hope. Suddenly, I could hardly wait for school to start. Hoping to avoid a repeat of my performance on the internship test, I inundated myself with the bible of every copy editor: The Associated Press stylebook. It had every hard and fast rule of fine editing, and I was determined to know every one of them by the time school started.

I was raring to go when September rolled around. My only fear was facing that empty dorm room again. The loneliness I felt when I went into that room still haunts my memory. It was as if the four walls swallowed me up.

I didn't stay in my room long enough for loneliness to set in. As soon as I got settled, I headed straight to the newsroom. I was anxious to get started. I wanted to thank Rick for recommending me for the job and to meet the new editor.

Renita wasn't at all the way I pictured her on the phone. She had long, flowing blond hair. She looked more like a movie star than a staunch newspaper editor.

Renita seemed friendly enough. She showed me around the newsroom and told me what I would be doing, and she introduced me to Nate Briles, the associate editor.

Nate was a freshman, straight out of high school. His fresh-faced, wiry visage made him look much more youthful. It was unusual for a freshman to work on the newspaper staff, let alone become associate editor. But then Nate was no usual freshman. He was editor of his high school paper and a gifted writer.

Nate and I hit it off from the beginning. There wasn't that barrier that existed with most people. He wanted to know about my disability, a subject that was taboo with most strangers. His candor startled me. I didn't mind talking about my disability, but no one had dared to ask about my handicap before.

It was the first time anyone had taken time to get to know me — the person. Nate listened intently as I told him how the palsy had left my taut limbs untamed and listless.

Once I had satisfied Nate's curiosity, the subject of my disability was put to rest and our talk turned to other things, namely journalism and our jobs on the paper. Our interest in the paper and love for writing drew us together. I left there that day feeling like I had known him forever.

The first weekend back at school, Rick invited the newspaper staff to his mountain cabin for the Labor Day weekend. I usually begged Dad to come get me on every long weekend, but this time was different. I wanted to be with my new friend.

As soon as classes let out on Friday, we headed for Colorado. It felt strange being with them, like I was out of place. I felt the way I had on the first day of kindergarten looking out at the unfamiliar faces.

I didn't stay a stranger long. Soon, I found myself sharing in the most intimate details of their lives. And I was talking about myself, something I seldom did among strangers. The long drive and open countryside gave us ample time to get to know one another, which was what Rick had hoped would happen by taking us on the retreat.

Over the next three days, I came to know the people who would become a family to me. Besides Renita and Nate, there was Heather Davis and Kenneth King. Heather was the only one I knew from the year before. She was in several of my journalism classes, but I had never talked to her before that weekend.

Kenneth was the newspaper photographer. He was a freshman and came to West Texas from Odessa, Nate's hometown. Kenneth and Nate were roommates.

It was a scenic drive through the hills and valleys into Colorado. I gazed out the window at the beauty of nature and all God created. The view of the mountains from Rick's cabin was breathtaking. The leaves were beginning to put on their fall brilliance. I'd never seen anything so beautiful and peaceful. Rick's mountain home was an authentic log cabin.

That night, while the rest of the group walked into town, Rick and I sat in the cool mountain air. It was a quiet night, and there was a brisk chill in the air. It was the first time I had had a quiet moment alone with Rick since school started, and I hadn't had a chance to properly thank him for getting me on the paper.

I spilled out a heartfelt thanks. Rick understood my intent and said kindly, "There's no need to thank me. You did it." He knew I was disappointed I didn't land the internship that summer. He was, too. But this was a new year.

"Forget about last year," he said. "Today is a new day. You're going to do fine."

I had come a long way in Rick's eyes since a year earlier, when he wondered if he should encourage me to pursue a career in journalism. Now, he boosted my confidence. He believed in me.

We rose before dawn the next morning, and Rick took us to watch the sun rise. It was an awesome sight, watching the sun peer from behind the mist-filled mountains.

Then, Rick took us up the mountain. He knew I'd have difficulty getting around on the uneven terrain. I offered to stay at the cabin while the others hiked. I didn't mind. I was just thrilled to be there. Rick wouldn't hear of leaving me at the cabin. Before we left school, Rick loaded my bicycle onto his truck and brought it along.

When we got to the foot of the mountain, he untied my bike and they began pushing me up the side of the mountain. It was about a half-mile uphill on a steep, rocky path. I never could have made it on foot. Even with my bike, I had trouble navigating along the narrow path.

Everyone helped me. Nate got on one side of me and Kenneth on the other, and together they pulled and tugged until we reached the top.

We came to a place where the ground leveled off and I could walk. I left the bike and walked across a grassy plain where the mountain peaked. This time, Renita and Heather helped me. They took my arms and led me through the thick brush.

It was the most spectacular view. It was a clear, sunny day, and I could see for miles across the rolling hills. I felt like I could reach up and touch heaven.

Rick stood before us with the sun coming over the hill as a backdrop. He gave us his sermon on the mount.

He told us the story of a young boy, brought up in the shanties of Oklahoma City. Growing up in a broken home, the boy was forced to do for himself at a tender age. He was a strapping lad and quite athletic. He turned all his attentiveness to sports, running track and cross-country. Running was his passion, often crowding out studying and book learning.

One day, a caring teacher sent for the young man. The boy walked in all covered in perspiration from having just come from practice. The teacher sat him down and began to impart to him the importance of hard work and studying, of reading and writing. She told him if he worked hard he could do anything he set his mind to.

That boy was Rick, and he remembered the lesson he learned that day. He began to set goals for himself and make them come true. Rick shared that message with us that day on the mountain.

"It doesn't matter what you want in life, you can do it if you set a goal and work to reach that goal," he said.

Rick told us to set our sights high — not to settle for second best. Anything worth having is worth fighting for, he said. Whether it's happiness or anything else, it takes commitment. I felt like his words were aimed straight at me.

"If you want to be a copy editor, work to be the best copy editor you can be," he said.

After Rick finished, he sent us off to spend time by ourselves and to think about the future. Sitting by myself atop the mountain, I felt closer to God than I ever had. I had time to ponder my future and think about what I wanted to do with my life.

I had let doubt fill my mind. I didn't know if I could do the job before me, but I had to believe. I set a goal that day: of being the best copy editor I could be.

Back at the cabin, everything was done for me. They catered to my every need. At mealtime, my meat was cut up for me before I asked that it be. It was a peaceful weekend. Even though I had known them only a few days, I felt so close to them.

That night, Renita shared her goals for the newspaper. She told us the expectations she had for each of us. She said the job would demand commitment, dedication and team work. It would take all of us working together, and she said some of us might not make it all the way through the semester. It wouldn't be easy, she told us. Then, she gave us a chance to change our minds, but no one did.

We were all new at the newspaper game. Except for Nate and Renita, none of us had done it before. No one was sure what to expect. I didn't know if I could do it, but

I was determined to try. I knew it wouldn't be easy. It never is, but I finally had the chance to prove myself.

I kept thinking about what Rick had said on the mountain. It made me start believing in myself. I started believing I could make something of my life. I really could do it. Rick was more than just an instructor that weekend. He taught me more than just about journalism; he taught me about life. He taught me to set goals for myself and then work to reach them.

We all had a great time that weekend, and no one wanted to leave. Classes resumed in full force the day after we got back, and the first issue of the newspaper was due out less than two weeks later.

It didn't leave much time. Stories had to be assigned and written. The stories had to be edited and the pages laid out. All of this and go to class. I never had taken an editing class, but I had to start proofreading stories for the paper. I hardly knew where to begin.

Rick was patient. As stories drifted in during the week, he went over each one of them with me. He edited them meticulously, explaining each change he made and showing me how to make the story flow smoothly from one thought to the next.

There was so much to remember and so many rules. I was overwhelmed. No wonder I had botched the editing test for the internship.

Rick and I worked side by side. We worked late into the evening and all weekend before the first paper came out.

Gradually, he let me begin editing the stories, and he watched. I was so careful, trying to catch every mistake, but Rick always found little slips of the pen I never even saw. I didn't think I'd ever get it, but Rick encouraged me.

Rick could edit a story in no time, while it took me 30 minutes to read a story. "You'll catch on," he assured me. "It just takes awhile. I've been at this a little longer than you have."

It gave me a sense of pride when the paper came out and I knew that I had a part in it. It made all the hard work seem worthwhile. Then, the long process began again.

I had little time to get lonely. I became so involved with the newspaper. It became my whole life. I loved it. I lived in the newsroom night and day the first two weeks of the semester. I hardly had time to go home weekends.

Rick soon relinquished the editing chores to my charge, and I edited all the copy. I had help, though. Renita and Heather helped. Then, there was Nate.

Nate and I were inseparable. We were together day and night. We did everything together. We often stayed and worked on newspaper assignments long after everyone else had gone home.

It wasn't all work, though. We did our share of carousing, too. Nate had a souped-up hot rod. It was a two-seater. After class, we'd climb in his old jalopy and take off. We'd ride carelessly for hours, often heading to Amarillo for the evening. We'd cruise through town, laughing and carrying on.

Nate was a real speed demon. He'd go flying down the expressway with the windows rolled down and the wind sweeping through the front seat and music blaring on the radio. It was invigorating. I forgot all my cares and worries when I was with Nate. It was a real contrast to my first year away from home, staying cooped up in my room all day. Finally, I was enjoying college life.

When the weather turned colder, Nate drove me to class. I pretended to be tough. "The cold doesn't bother me," I told him. "I can ride my bike." But Nate wouldn't hear of it. He insisted on driving me. I was glad he did.

It was a frigid winter, much colder than the year before. The first snow of the season came in late October. Temperatures had been hovering below freezing all week, and I knew it was only a matter of time before we got our first winter blast.

I dreaded the snow because it made getting around difficult at best. The inevitable finally came. I had a night class one night a week, and it started sleeting while I was in class. By the end of class, there was a thin blanket of snow glistening on the ground.

It wasn't a heavy snow, but it was enough that the instructor let class out early. The roads were getting slick, so the instructor offered to drive me home.

The kind teacher was always looking out for me. She often sounded like my mother, telling me to be sure and bundle up and wear my mittens. She worried about me riding home in the snow that night. It was snowing pretty hard when I got ready to leave. The instructor told me to leave my bike there and let her take me back to my room.

But I wouldn't listen. I insisted on riding my bike. People were walking from class, and if they could make it, I could, too. I bundled up in my heavy coat and stocking cap and set out.

I had no trouble at first. I sloshed through the sleet and over the snow-covered walkways. I had good traction. My bike didn't get stuck as I had thought it might. As long as it was just snow, I made it fine.

About half way home, I hit a patch of ice. I gently tapped the brake, and the bike began to slide. I slowed down to keep control of the bike. The wind started picking up, and snow was blowing in my face. I couldn't see what was ahead, but I plunged ahead. I was almost there. I was rounding the corner when the bike slid off the sidewalk.

I skidded off onto the soft snow. I tried to push myself back onto the sidewalk, but I couldn't move. I was stuck. Each time I put my feet down to propel myself back onto the sidewalk, I would slip and lose my footing. It was like walking on glass; I couldn't keep my balance.

The wind was howling now. I couldn't see anything. If anyone came out of the building, they wouldn't be able to see me through the snow. The thought of being stranded there all night ran through my mind, but I wasn't worried. Not yet anyway. I knew it was only a matter of time before someone came along and spotted me. The only thing I could do was wait.

My hands were numb. I had been out there only a few minutes. I knew I wasn't going to freeze. Finally, one of the guys from the dorm came up on his way back from class. He rushed over to rescue me.

"Boy, I'm glad to see you," I said.

He pulled me out of the snow drift and started pushing me up to the building. As he rolled me in out of the cold, the warm air hit me across the face, but my hands were still numb. I couldn't hold the key to get into my room. He unlocked the door and helped me into my room.

It snowed all night and all the next day. It was the biggest blizzard of the year. Classes were canceled the next day. The cold lingered for several days, and I relied on Nate to pick me up and drive me to class.

As soon as the ground began to thaw, I was back out on my three-wheeler. My bike gave me a sense of independence. People saw my bike, and they knew I couldn't be far away.

As the weeks went on, I spent more time at the paper and less time studying. I took two more writing classes that semester. I became wholly absorbed in the newspaper.

I felt overwhelmed at times. Each week, Renita would set another mountain of papers before me, and I faced the insuperable task of uncovering the hidden fallacies. It seemed hopeless. By the end of the week, my eyes were swimming in a sea of words. I never would have made it through the semester were it not for the kindness and support of Nate and the others on the staff.

We had weekly critique sessions of our work. The journalism instructors, Rick and Billy Smith, marked up the paper. They highlighted all the mistakes they could find in red ink. Some weeks, there was more red than black.

It was hard for me to accept their criticism of my work. I had doubts about being there anyway, wondering if my work was really satisfactory or if they merely tolerated me. I thought every mistake was my fault. It was my job to catch the mistakes, I told myself.

I accepted their criticism gracefully and openly, but privately I felt as if I had failed. My emotions swayed between moments of joy and sadness. I often became depressed when things didn't go right, but I kept my feelings of insecurity inside.

Gradually, I learned to take their faultfinding in the manner in which it was offered. No one thought I was incapable as I had imagined. They only wanted to help me.

I soon began to take on more responsibility at the paper, writing editorials and making more decisions. I loved every minute of it. Finally, I was doing what I always had dreamed of doing.

My Big Break

❦

The new year brought change and a few surprises into our lives. As I was preparing to return to school from the Christmas break, the country was preparing for war with Iraq, the first massive call to arms in my lifetime.

The country was turned topsy-turvy as families braced to send husbands and wives, sons and daughters to war. Talk of the war terrified me. Not knowing what would happen with the war, I was nervous about leaving my family and returning to school.

I knew I would never have to fight in a war because of my disability, but for friends in the Army Reserves, war was a real possibility. One friend from church already had left for the Persian Gulf, and others were put on alert.

Everyone was on edge, knowing that at any moment a bomb could explode that would change our lives forever. There was an air of uncertainty for many students, not knowing if they would get to stay in school or have to fight in the war.

The only comforting thought about returning to school was knowing that Nate would be there. I could hardly wait to see him again.

I was one of the first students to return to the dorm after the Christmas break. The halls were hauntingly quiet. That night, I rode my bike around the still-deserted campus. It was strange to see the streets so empty, no loud music blaring out of dorm-room windows.

It was like a ghost town. I was riding aimlessly through the desolate streets, searching for a familiar face, when I spotted Rick coming out of the journalism building. He saw me across the parking lot and began wildly waving me toward the building.

He was beaming with excitement. I had never seen him so worked up. As I rode up, Rick began shouting, "They're here! They're here!"

"What's here?" I asked.

Rick rushed me into the building, to the top of the stairs, where stacks of empty boxes were piled up to the ceiling, and a row of shiny new computers sat on a table.

We had been anxiously awaiting the arrival of new computers since I started to WT a year and a half earlier. Rick was eager to demonstrate the new wizardry. They had the latest technology with all the bells and whistles.

Then, Rick hit me with an even bigger surprise.

"Renita quit!" he said with the same enthusiasm as he told me about the computers. It was no secret that Rick and Renita had had their differences. I had even had a few run-ins with her.

I was shocked. "Who's going to be the editor?" I asked.

"We have to hire someone," he said. "I think you should apply."

Me? Surely he was joking, I thought. I could never be editor. Could I? A sudden burst of excitement exploded inside me and raced up my spine as for one brief moment, I considered what it would be like. Me, editor of the college newspaper!

Soon, my senses returned, and I quickly came down to reality. "I don't know," I said. "There are others more qualified. What about Nate?" Nate had much more experience than I did.

"Well, Nate's still a freshman. He'll have plenty of time to be editor . . . after you're gone," Rick said.

"I don't know." I'd never thought about being editor. I was thrilled just to work on the newspaper. I never dreamed I could be editor. I thought someday, perhaps my senior year, maybe . . . But not now. I wasn't ready.

"Think about it," Rick said. "You would be a great editor."

That was all that was said about the matter for the moment. That evening after I left Rick, I didn't want to go back to my barren room. I kept riding, roaming aimlessly through the streets that now were dimly lighted. Farther and farther away from campus, I rode. I found myself on a darkened street far from campus, and as I watched the sun collide with the landscape, I remembered what Rick had once said. "You can be anything you want to be, if you only try."

I had always been a follower, never a leader. I doubted my ability to be a leader. I knew with my slurred mouthings, it would be difficult to communicate with the staff. But from somewhere deep in my heart, a feeling of hope welled up inside me. Could I really be the editor? Could I really do it? I had to try.

I raced back to campus with increasing speed, the sky now swallowed up by darkness. I rarely strayed that far from campus and never at night. My heart was beating wildly as I reached my room.

I lay in bed that night, my eyes wide open, thinking about the night's events. I should have been thinking about starting class the next morning, but my mind kept wandering back to my conversation with Rick.

Nate returned to school the next day. I could hardly wait to see him and tell him the big news.

We had a rollicking reunion. When I saw him in the bookstore that afternoon, I bolted across the room to greet him. I was sure Nate already had heard about Renita. When I caught up with him, we both began talking at once.

We stood in the middle of the store, laughing and tittering like a couple of hyenas. People were staring at us like we had lost our minds. I didn't care, though. I was elated to see Nate again. When I was with him, nothing else mattered.

I quickly forgot my fears about the fighting going on half way across the world. We must have carried on for the better part of an hour. Finally, Nate said, "I hear you're going to be the new editor."

"Who told you that?" I asked.

"Rick. He said you were all excited about it."

"I haven't decided if I'm going to do it," I said, knowing full well that I'd already made up my mind to apply. "Besides, someone else might get the job. What about you? Aren't you going to apply?"

"I wouldn't get it. You'll get it. I know you will."

I left with those words ringing in my ears. I could hardly concentrate on my studies that afternoon. I was too worked up. All I could think about was becoming editor.

We had another reunion that evening when Nate and Jessica came to my room to watch television. The three of us had a lot to catch up on after the Christmas break.

Jessica was an editor for the yearbook and wrote for the paper. She was a year younger than me. Nate had a crush on Jessica and had had since the day he met her. He would never admit it, but there were the telltale signs. The way he looked at her with those big puppy-dog eyes when she walked into the room, the way she giggled whenever Nate told a joke.

Our happy reunion came to a sudden and abrupt halt when one of the fellows who lived upstairs stormed into my room with the news that American troops had launched an air attack on Iraq. He came in ranting and raving about the invasion, then as suddenly as he appeared, he was off to tell others.

I turned on the television, and we learned that the United States was at war with Iraq. It was January 16, 1991, a night I'll never forget. It was a sad day when our country began fighting another. We sat in horror as we watched the news reports. We heard the rumble of bombs exploding in the distance as a quaking voice on the television described what was happening.

Images of war flashed before us as the fighting was played out on the screen. Brilliant streaks of light illuminated the night sky over Baghdad; there was the distinct crackle of gun fire. Suddenly, a cold, void feeling came over me. I felt hollow inside.

I looked at Jessica. I could tell she was frightened. A single teardrop streaked down her face. She stared intently at the television. She had a friend in Saudi Arabia and feared for his safety. Nate reached over and took her hand to try to reassure her.

We were all frightened. We sat motionless, our eyes fixed on the screen. No one said a word. We just sat there and, like the rest of the nation, stared helplessly at the set.

Nate and Jessica stayed until midnight, then Nate walked her to her room. She was still pretty shook up when they left my room.

The next day, it was all anybody could talk about. Professors devoted their classes to talking about the war, and students gathered to pray for the soldiers. The radio was on in the newsroom when I arrived at the paper. Nate was talking to Rick and Billy about the war. They said we should do something. We all wanted to do our part. Rick suggested that we put out a special war edition. He said he would talk to his classes the next day for anyone who wanted to help with the special edition.

The newsroom soon was abuzz with activity. Everyone was scurrying about, talking to people and trying to get reactions to the war, and in between listening to updates on the skirmishes in Iraq.

Nate became acting editor until a new chief could be selected. Nate quickly took charge with story and picture assignments. We would have to hustle to get the paper out by Tuesday night, only four days away.

Patriotism began to spread like wild fire. All across campus, patriotism was alive with yellow ribbons streaming from trees and cars adorned with red, white and blue ribbons, a sign of hope. Flags waved freely at buildings on campus to show support for the troops.

The most striking display of support was the messages of encouragement painted on the car windshields and dorm-room windows. Signs reading "God bless America" and "We support the troops" showed hope and concern for the soldiers in the Gulf. I was proud to be an American.

Emotions ran high that week. I interviewed students and faculty for a story about those who had family and friends in the Gulf. The university's vice president was a lieutenant colonel in the Air Force Reserves and had a son on a plane headed for Saudi Arabia. He said he could have as little as 24-hours notice to report for duty if he received his orders.

We worked feverishly that weekend. Everyone pitched in and helped. Students gave up their weekend to help with the edition. I worked on my story most of the weekend. There was little time to think about anything else. Still, my mind raced ahead to Monday and my interview with the publications board. I found myself thinking more and more about becoming editor.

My fiercest competitor in the race was Heather Davis. She was a strong person, full of confidence. It was awkward that weekend working so closely together. We traded snide glances, the way a fighter peers at an opponent before he steps into the ring.

All weekend, Heather made surly remarks like, "When I become editor ..." Of course, I got in my jabs, too. I strutted into the room informing everyone, "I would be in my office," gesturing to the room now vacated by Renita. It was half in jest, but I took the competition seriously. Nate joined the race after all. Although he was still a freshman, he said the tryout would prepare him for a day when he might become the editor.

The Interview

I was nervous about speaking before the publications board. If the board couldn't understand me, they might think I was unable to communicate clearly with others. I rehearsed my speech to the board, speaking slowly and distinctly.

Fearing that I would become flustered and start spouting some unintelligible language, I recorded my responses on my Touch Talker. I simply had to type the words into a computer, and a synthesized voice would repeat my words on command.

I got the Touch Talker on loan from the education service center in Amarillo while I was in college. It was portable, so I could carry it with me to class. I often used the machine in class and when I interviewed others for stories.

My legs trembled as I made my way, Touch Talker in tow, to the dean's office for my interview. There, a panel of professors, newspaper professionals and students would grill me with questions. Heather was in with the board when I arrived. I would be next. My hands began shaking uncontrollably as I waited to go in.

My chief objective was to impress the board. It stood for one thing in my mind: proving to others — and to myself — that I was capable. Whenever I wanted to impress someone, my coordination deserted me. I wondered how I would ever make it the 100 yards into the room without losing my balance. I wondered if the board would pity me, or if they would question whether it was a good idea for someone as handicapped as I was to be the editor.

Finally, I saw Heather appear from behind the closed door. She shot me one final snarl as she passed me and left the office. I wasn't going to be moved by her ploys to psyche me out. It was time for me to go in. I mustered up all the strength I had to make it across the small office.

Rick pointed me to a chair at the end of a long table. I was relieved to see some familiar faces in the room. Rick was seated at the other end of the table. He offered me a reassuring look as if to say, "You're going to do fine. Don't worry." I couldn't help but be nervous, though. I was terrified.

I looked around the room and saw another friendly face, Carol Snowden. Carol had been the yearbook editor when I was on the staff the year before. I felt a little better after seeing Carol. She was familiar with my writing and knew what I could do.

Then, the interrogation began. The board began firing questions at me. Rick threw out the first question: "What do you think the role of the student newspaper is?"

I sat silent for a moment. Every eye in the room was trained on me. Beneath the table, my legs were quaking like a creaking rocking chair. I thought for a minute longer, then slowly and distinctly, began to speak.

It was my chance to share my passion for the First Amendment. I saw the newspaper as a way to share ideas, to express opinions. The First Amendment is a sacred freedom entrusted not just to journalists, but to every American. With the war, the freedom to speak became even more real to me.

One by one, each panelist took a turn in the interrogation. "What is your view on censorship?" "What should the editorial policy be?" "What role should the adviser play in running the newspaper?" I answered each question frankly and directly, even though I knew some of my answers disagreed with some of Rick's views.

I sensed that some of the panelists were having trouble understanding me as I struggled to get the words out, but no one asked me to repeat myself. I guess they were afraid to ask me to repeat. I gave my responses slowly, distinctly, and without the aid of the Touch Talker.

Afterward, one of the members seemed disappointed that I didn't use the Touch Talker. He wanted to see how the computer worked, but I felt I must speak for myself to show them I could do it on my own.

My hair was ringing with perspiration when I left the interview, but I had made it. I made it through the interview without stammering. All I had to do now was make it to the door without stumbling, and I'd have it made. I thanked the board and walked stiffly toward the door.

Nate was in the office when I came out. "How did it go?" he asked.

"I don't know," I said.

"You're going get it," he said assuringly. "I might as well not even go in."

"No, you'll get it. Good luck in your interview."

As I walked slowly back to the newsroom, I was so relieved the interview was over, I didn't care who the board selected. I had given it my best try, now whatever happened, I had tried.

Heather was in the newsroom when I arrived. She was actually cordial. She even smiled when I came in. She asked how the interview went. I don't know what brought about the sudden change in demeanor. I guess she thought now that the interviews were over, there was no need to keep up the animosities. All we could do now was wait.

We talked about the questions when Nate came in. "Hi, guys," he said. He didn't look nervous at all. He was his usual, cheerful self.

The only thing left now was to wait for Rick to return with the verdict. We didn't talk. We sat motionless, staring up at the clock.

After what seemed like hours, Rick appeared at the door. He called the three of us into his office for the answer we had all been waiting for. My knocking knees shook violently as I got up and started toward the door. My heart was pounding and felt as if it was about to explode.

I grappled my way into the office and sank into the chair closest to the door to give me support before I fell down. This was it. I had prepared myself for the possibility that I wouldn't get it, that they would choose Heather or Nate. Still, I hoped and prayed it would be my name Rick called out.

Rick followed us into the room and took a seat behind a desk cluttered with books and stacks of old, faded newspapers. He gave a sly grin as if to agonize us a little longer. Then, he began.

He started by saying the board felt that any of us would make a good editor. He said he hoped that we would all work together for the good of the newspaper, no matter who was chosen.

"But," he said, "there can only be one editor." He paused for what seemed like an eternity. Then, it happened. "The board has selected you, Chris."

My heart did a flip in my chest. For a minute, I thought I had heard wrong. I couldn't believe it. Suddenly, everyone was gathering around me. Nate slapped me on the back. "Way to go, dog!" he said.

Rick came over and shook my hand. "I know you'll do a great job."

Even Heather congratulated me in her own jeering way. "Looks like you got me," she said punching on the shoulder with her fist. She obviously was disappointed, but she took it well.

All the reporters had gathered in the newsroom for the announcement. Nate ran from the room to give everybody the news.

Everyone began applauding and cheering when I came into the room. The reporters all gathered around me. I was overwhelmed by all the attention. One by one, they congratulated me. It was truly one of the happiest days of my life.

Editor-in-Chief

It was only after I learned that Nate told the publications board he wanted me to have the job that I realized what a true friend he was. I would be a senior next year, and he still had three years to become the editor.

It was my time now, Nate said, and he promised to help me any way he could. I never had anyone do anything like that for me before. He was a true friend.

As the day wore on, the excitement began to die down as the crowd broke up and everyone went back to class. But in my heart, the excitement was still burning.

In all the excitement, I nearly forgot about the fighting on the other side of the world. The war raged on despite the triumph in my life, and we had less than a day left to get out the special edition.

That evening, Nate and Jessica surprised me with a cake to celebrate my new position. Heather didn't stay around for the celebration. She was obviously disappointed that she didn't get the job herself and was not in the mood for a party.

In the excitement of the day, I hadn't thought to call Mom and Dad to tell them the news. When Rick found out I hadn't told them, he insisted that I call right then.

It was late when I called, and the first thing Mom thought when she answered the phone was that something must be wrong. Why else would I be calling so late?

"Nothing's wrong," I assured her. "Everything's right. I got the job. I'm the editor."

The phone line was silent for a minute. "That's wonderful, son," she said finally through faint sobs. "We're proud of you."

When I had told my parents I was thinking about applying, they were skeptical. They were afraid I'd be taking on more than I could handle and that my school work might suffer. But they did nothing to discourage me. They said it was my decision. Now that I had it, they were overjoyed. I had crossed another milestone in my parents' eyes. I had my first job.

I went right back to work after I got off the phone with Mom. Nate and I worked long after everyone else had gone home. We worked into the early-morning hours on the special edition, and it was nearly 2 when I got back to my room.

I was exhausted. I lay in the bed that night not fully realizing what had happened that day. I am the editor, I kept telling myself. I thanked God for what he had done for me that day. My dream was becoming a reality. I asked the Lord to help me, knowing in my own strength I could do nothing, but in him everything was possible.

The next morning, I was up at dawn and back at the newsroom putting the finishing touches on the special edition. Our deadline was noon, which we missed by almost seven hours.

I saw this as my first failure as the new editor. Deadlines are critical in newspapers, and I missed my first one. Despite glitches in the new computer system that caused part of the delay and the fact that Nate was the only one who knew how to use the new machines, I saw the missed deadline as a reflection on my ability. I was stubbornly determined not to fail.

Even though others considered me capable of being a strong editor, because of my handicap I felt that I had to prove myself in everything I did. I concentrated everything in me on impressing Rick and my staff.

The next few days and weeks were a tide of emotions for me. I had such a sense of pride when the first papers rolled off the press and I saw my name in the editor's box. Everywhere I went on campus, people greeted me and congratulated me on becoming the editor. I got calls and letters from people commending us on the job we did on the war edition.

I couldn't take credit for that, though. Most of it was finished before I took over. Still, things were good. I was ready to conquer the world.

I began making decisions on what stories to print and what issues to cover. My confidence was improving. I took a hard editorial stance in the next edition, sparking some controversy when I came out in favor of the decision to cut football from the university. It was an unpopular stand, despite the fact that athletics was putting a financial strain on the school.

I received more phone calls and letters, only this time they weren't praising my work, but disagreeing with me. I accepted this criticism. I knew people would disagree with me. I had prepared myself for this criticism.

I stood my ground when a faculty member threatened legal action after I printed comments he made about the war. He was the ROTC commander, and as such, was forbidden to talk publicly about the war. But when he spoke to a group of students on campus about the Army maneuvers, I felt it was my duty to write about it.

He was furious when I wrote a front-page article for the next week's paper. He was on the phone to Rick, demanding to know how he could allow me to print the article. I was relieved when Rick defended me, saying I had a right to report on his lecture.

Things went well for the first few weeks. Everyone seemed pleased with my work. Rick even praised my editorials in our critique sessions. I had a real sense of pride when we had a good paper, but I could always feel it when it didn't come out the way I had planned. I got a sick feeling down deep in my heart.

After a few weeks, things really began to shake. People started complaining that the paper wasn't giving some groups on campus fair coverage. They wanted to know why we wrote stories about some groups and not others.

I began to feel like I was in over my head. I tried to be a fair editor, but things got overlooked and people complained. I quickly discovered there was more to being editor than just writing and editing. I had to learn to be a leader. It was hard for me because I'd always been a follower, never a leader. I depended on Nate more than ever. I took advantage of him sometimes, assigning him stories I didn't want to do. He never complained. He was always right by my side.

I had to prove to Rick that he hadn't made a mistake in recommending me for the job. Nothing else mattered.

I got less and less enjoyment out of writing. My emotions were on edge all the time. I took every criticism of the paper as though it was aimed at me. I was the editor, and I was responsible. I became depressed. I dreaded Monday morning and the thought of having to put out another paper.

Nate knew something was wrong. I walked around in a daze. I wasn't the usual enthusiastic, hopeful person I normally was. I tried to hide my feelings, but Nate could see my frustrations. It must have been written on my face. He tried to get me to open up and talk about what was wrong, but I pushed him away.

Then, at the most awkward time, all these feelings gushed out. We had just finished another edition, and I was in my cubby-hole office reading the paper. Rick and a few reporters were in the newsroom looking at the papers when suddenly Rick shouted, "Chris! Why are the names wrong on these pictures?"

I bolted from my chair and rushed into the newsroom, fearing I had messed up again.

"Where?" I asked in a state of panic.

Rick grinned. "Not really. I was just seeing if you were awake in there."

A fit of rage ignited inside me. I turned around and stormed back into my office and burst into tears.

"He's really upset, isn't he?" Rick asked as he started toward my door. I turned my face to the wall to hide the tears. I couldn't let him see me crying like a baby. At that moment, I felt as if the whole world was falling in on me. I got a hollow, sunken feeling in my chest.

Rick came over and gently put his hand on my shoulder. "I was only joking. Everything's all right," he said.

I tried to stop crying, but a steady stream of tears kept rolling down my cheeks. Nate and the reporters were gathered around the door, gawking at me. I was humiliated. I wanted to run away.

"It's all right to cry," Rick said. He brushed everyone away from the door and came back and patted me on the shoulder again. I never felt more like a failure than at that moment. For Rick to see me crying, he must have thought I was such a weakling.

He sat on the edge of the desk while I let it all out. "It's all right," he kept saying. But it wasn't all right. I had let him down and made a fool out of myself in front of my staff.

Finally, when I calmed down and stopped bawling, Rick tried to comfort me, saying he knew the pressure I was under. I had never been in a position where I had so much responsibility.

He told me to go home and get some rest. I would feel better in the morning, he assured me. I didn't see how things could get any better by morning, and I left that day believing that I could never recover from this.

When I went back to the newsroom the next day, I tried to slink in unnoticed. I slipped into my office and closed the door. I didn't want anyone to see me. I hid out in my office most of the morning.

It was midmorning before anyone noticed I was there. Rick finally noticed my light on and came in to see how I was doing. We had a long talk. I was ready to quit right then. At least that way I wouldn't have to face the staff again. What they must have thought about me.

I had fallen behind in my studies, too. Finally, the pressure of trying to balance three writing classes and be editor had taken its toll on me. I thought the best thing for everyone would be for me to quit. I had never been a quitter, but I didn't think I could face Nate and the staff again.

Rick wouldn't let me quit. "You can't let the pressure get to you," he said. "It's never going to be easy, but you have to go on. You're strong. You have to keep going."

After that, everyone was careful around me, probably afraid that I would go off again. Nate tried to lessen the burden by taking on more of the work. I felt guilty that he had to do so much, but he never seemed to mind. He never complained. Even Rick and Billy let up a little in the critiques. They were a little gentler in their reproofs.

We saw our share of successes that year, too. The paper received an All American Award from the Associated Collegiate Press, one of only 12 college newspapers in the country to win the award. One writer on the staff received national recognition for writing the top college journalism story. It was the Pulitzer of college awards for the writer. Her story uncovered the university's stock purchase without approval from the board of regents.

We saw a new university president sworn in that year, and I had the task of interviewing the new president.

It was times like that that kept me going. It invigorated me. And knowing that I had a part in leading the paper through one of the most historic years in the school's history — it made all the sweat and effort seem worth it.

As the semester neared an end, I started thinking about the summer. I didn't want to go back home. I desperately wanted to find a job, and Rick was determined to help me get an internship.

A large media group came to the school in the spring, interviewing people for a summer intern program. Rick arranged for me to meet with the recruiters. I thought the experience from the past year would have made me better prepared for the interview, unlike the year before when I tried for the editing job.

I was desperate for a job, so when they asked if I was willing to move away from my family, I told them I would. I didn't know how I would survive apart from my parents, but I'd find a way. I would have done anything for the chance to work.

The recruiters seemed impressed with my work, or so I thought. I showed them samples of my writing, and Rick gave me a glowing recommendation. The recruiters talked favorably in the interview, and I came out certain that they would offer me a job, hopefully at one of the papers in the area.

For weeks afterward, I lived with expectancy. They had to hire me, I told myself. I waited for the phone to ring. When Rick finally got the call a few weeks before school was out, I was disappointed once again.

I was standing outside Rick's office and overheard him talking to the recruiter. I knew I shouldn't have been eavesdropping, but I had to know. I heard the whole conversation. They had a job for one writer on our staff, but none for me.

Rick pleaded my case with the woman on the phone. "What about Chris?" he asked. "Yes, but if you'd just give him a chance . . ."

There was a minute of silence. My pulse was racing.

"But I know he can do it . . ."

This exchange continued for a few more minutes. Then, I heard Rick hang up the phone. It was over, and I didn't get the job. I ran back to the newsroom, feeling like I was at the end of my rope. I was never going to get a job.

Rick came out shortly with the bad news. I pretended to be ignorant about his phone conservation. He told me I didn't get the internship because the editors didn't think I could handle the rigorous physical demands of the job, rushing out to cover an accident or event and then back to the newsroom to pound out a story.

I tried to put up a tough front, pretend it didn't matter, but deep down I was crushed. Rick was just angry. It's hard to say who was more disappointed, Rick or me for he truly wanted me to find success.

The joy of learning that I was selected to continue as editor for another year was buffered by news that Rick was leaving West Texas in the fall. He had accepted another job at the University of Hawaii. I only saw it that he was leaving me.

I was devastated. I would be lost without Rick. In the two years that I knew Rick, he had been more than a teacher to me. He had become a friend who had sustained me through many toils and sorrows. I knew God had brought him into my life.

How could God take him away now, when I had another year of school left? He couldn't leave yet. But as the final days of that year quickly approached, I found myself having to say good-bye to a man who had changed my life.

It was a tearful farewell as I reached out to shake Rick's hand and thank him for what he had given me. He kept me from giving up. He could never know how much he taught me; he gave me the courage to believe in myself.

I returned to Pampa that summer despite wanting to stay at school. Without a job, I had to return home. It was a time of uncertainty, not knowing what would happen when I went back in the fall. I was afraid. After being rejected so many times by editors, I was afraid the new adviser wouldn't give me a chance as Rick had.

Not knowing who the new adviser would be, my mind ran through all kinds of scenarios. I was afraid he would consider me incompetent and try to have me replaced with an able-bodied editor. I would have to prove myself all over again. I didn't know what was going to happen, but I knew one thing. God had brought me that far. He wouldn't let me fall now.

Leaning on God

Soon after I returned to Pampa, the Texas Rehabilitation Commission told me it was going to buy me a computer to use my senior year. The state agency had paid my tuition and books my first two years at West Texas. But my counselor in rehab, like everyone else, balked at my chances for making it all the way through college. He wasn't optimistic that someone with my limitations would be able to find work if I did graduate. I have to prove myself to yet another doubter.

I had to see the counselor once a semester and take a copy of my grades to chart my progress and qualify for the financial aid. Each semester when I handed him my records, he scratched his head as he looked down the row of all A's. Mr. Howell just shook his head and told me to keep up the progress. Still, he doubted.

That semester when I went to see Mr. Howell, he had some good news for me. He said not only was the state going to pick up my tuition, it was going to pay for my room, meals and, at the urging of Rick, it was going to buy me a computer.

Mr. Howell said once they saw what I could do and my accomplishment on becoming editor, they realized I wasn't a risk like they thought I was. They realized they could have done more to help me. And when school started, I would receive a check each week to pay for personal items.

I was elated by their confidence. I wouldn't be such a burden on Mom and Dad. I helped with expenses when I could, but they had paid all my bills since I started college at Clarendon.

I got the computer early in June. A Macintosh Portable, the same kind we used on the newspaper. This would cut down on the late hours and all-night writing sessions I put in at the newsroom.

The computer helped me forget my worries, at least for a while, and the uncertainty that lingered with the search for a new adviser. I started working almost immediately after I got the computer on ideas for the paper. I was determined to have everything organized by the time school started so nothing would be overlooked again.

I would show the new adviser that I was organized. I made new style sheets and typed up schedules for writers so no one would have an excuse for missing a deadline. I was going to impress the new adviser by showing him I had everything ready when school started. He wouldn't have a chance to reject me.

I stayed in close contact with Nate over the summer. I called him every few weeks with new plans for the paper. I must have made him crazy.

We planned to return to school a week early to begin making preparations for our first edition. As it got closer and closer for time to go back to school, I became more excited. I believed that God would provide an answer to all my worries.

Two weeks before school started, Nate called me with more bad news. "I'm sorry to let you down pal, but I'm not coming back to school," he said. My heart became heavy, like a load of bricks had fallen on me.

Nate was offered a job as a youth minister at his church. And he was going to take it. "I believe this is what God wants me to do," he said.

"Then, that's what you need to do," I said, trying to hold back the tears.

Nate had known about the job for several weeks but put off telling me because he knew I would be disappointed. "I'm sorry to let you down," he kept saying.

I was devastated. I ran out of the house, jumped on my bike and began peddling as hard as I could, tears streaming down my face. Mom and Dad didn't know what was wrong. I just ran out.

I rode down the street, barely able to see from the tears in my eyes. I sped around the corner and across a field to the back of the junior high, still deserted for the summer. No one could see me there. I poured my heart out to God.

I felt like everyone was deserting me, first Rick and now Nate. One by one, people were leaving me. I knew God had a reason for taking them away, though I didn't understand. God began to show me all I really needed was him. I had to stretch my faith and believe in him to help me.

All my life, I had looked to man for answers to my problems. I relied on my parents to provide everything when I was growing up. When I got to college, I tried to do everything myself — or else I looked to others to help me. I didn't give God a chance.

God was teaching me to draw my strength from him. Like the manna rained from heaven, he would provide what

I needed now. Sometimes, I think God took all these people out of my life to show me he was in control. He would never leave me. He would be my strength.

When I finally went home and told Mom and Dad about Nate leaving, they didn't understand. They assured me everything would turn out all right. I had told them nothing about the problems I had at school. They didn't understand why I was so upset. They told me I had to get up and keep going.

The next day, I called Billy Smith, the only instructor remaining in the journalism program. School was just weeks always, and I had no associate editor. "What am I going to do?" I asked. Billy reminded me it was my job to hire the staff. Just get somebody else, he said.

He suggested two names for me to consider. One was a transfer student from a junior college; the other was a writer already on the staff, Charee Godwin.

I didn't know the transfer student very well. I had met her only once, when she came to visit the school. I knew what I had to do.

Charee was thrilled when I called to offer her the job. I told Charee I'd be returning to school in a week and asked her to meet me there early in the week to discuss ideas for the paper.

One crisis resolved, I could concentrate fully on trying to make a good impression on the new adviser. In my conversation with Billy, he told me the new adviser would start Monday, the day I was to return.

Billy told me that Dave Wohlfarth was a veteran newspaper editor and would bring a lot of experience to the journalism program. But that only served to confirm my worries. If other editors had rejected me, I was sure he would, too.

Pressing On

All the changes and uncertainty made returning to school that year harder than all the ones before it. It was even harder than leaving home the first time, when I didn't know what to expect but knew my parents would welcome me back with loving arms if I failed.

It was my final year in college, the last year before I would be thrown into the reality of the working world. I couldn't quit now. I had to reach the finish line.

I arrived on campus a week before classes began. I wanted time to organize my ideas and get ready for the first edition. I was determined that things would be different this year. I would be a strong leader, efficient and organized. Nothing would get overlooked again.

I got settled in my room, then headed for the newsroom. I saddled up on my bike and began the trip I had made a hundred times before, only to find when I got there that everything had changed. There were new faces and new people. People I didn't even know were milling around the newsroom, the room I had run just months before.

When I reached the newsroom at the top of the stairs, I saw a light on in what had been Rick's office. Thinking the new adviser already had started work for the day, I gathered up my strength and began the long walk across the newsroom to his office. But the room was empty. The office looked strangely empty, void of the stacks of faded newspapers Rick had had scattered around the room.

I turned around to see Billy Smith, one familiar face among a sea of no names. He told me Dave had gone out and would be back soon. I walked to my office on the other side of the newsroom and began sorting through the stacks of mail that had collected over the summer.

My heart was racing as I waited for the stranger to come through the door. What if he won't give me a chance, I asked myself. I stared at the door, my heart galloping like a team of wild horses.

Finally, I saw him come in. He headed into his office. I sat paralyzed for a few seconds more, then began walking across the newsroom.

Dave looked like what I thought a newspaper editor should look like. He had graying hair and thick reading glasses. The embers of a freshly extinguished cigar glowed brightly in an astray on the desk.

He seemed startled when I entered the room. I introduced myself, extending my hand toward his.

"Oh yes, Billy has told me quite a lot about you," he said motioning me into his office.

I was relieved. At least Billy had warned him about me so it wasn't a total shock when I came waddling through the door. We talked for a few minutes. He told me about his experiences working as an editor in Dayton, Ohio. Then, he began asking about me and my work on the school paper.

As I began to tell him about my new ideas and show him the things I had worked on during the summer, a strange look came on his face. He scratched his head, and I could tell he hadn't understood a word I had said. I tried to say each word slowly and distinctly, but he couldn't make out my garbled words. He kept asking me to repeat things.

I began to get frustrated, making my speech even more unintelligible. It was normal for strangers to have trouble understanding me, but he seemed to have more trouble than others.

We talked a little while longer, then I rose to leave. Dave reached out to shake my hand again and said he looked forward to working with me, but I could tell he felt uneasy, too. We weren't communicating, and in our business, that was crucial.

I went back to my office to prepare for the staff meeting I had called for the next day. My nerves settled a little after my meeting with Dave. At least he hadn't dismissed me altogether. Despite the communication gap, he seemed willing to give me a chance. That's all I wanted: a chance. If I failed, I failed but at least I tried.

I realized that the next few weeks would be my toughest challenge yet. I was in charge now. It was all on my shoulders. Before, I had relied on Nate to pull me through, but now I had to take charge.

My first chance to demonstrate this came the next day at the staff meeting. I had requested that all my editors meet me a few days before classes began to plan the first edition of the paper. I wanted to show Dave that I had initiative to get things started even before the semester began.

Except for Randal McGavock, the sports editor, everyone was new to the staff. This made my job even harder because I felt I not only had to prove myself to Dave, but to them as well. But I plowed in to let everyone know right from the beginning that I was a leader.

Everyone gathered in the newsroom, and I began to lay out my goals for the newspaper, much as Renita had explained her expectations for the paper at Rick's cabin a year earlier.

Dave still was not understanding me. He had a far-away look on his face as if he was having doubts about whether I'd be able to communicate well enough with the other staff members. The students understood me much better than he had at first and interpreted my jumbled sentences to him.

I handed out a list of story ideas I had worked on over the summer and gave my staff its first assignments. I had high expectations of my staff. Expecting them to come in before the summer break was officially over was asking a lot. I thought if I had the determination and dedication to start, everyone else should, too.

By the time classes started the following week, I had written a story and an editorial for the first edition, which was still a week away. Things were going well as I tried to convince myself that I could get by without Nate. I began to draw my strength from God instead of man. I prayed each day and asked God to help me, realizing without him I could do nothing. God was faithful and helped me through the early days of that semester.

It wasn't until I gave Dave my first story to read that his doubts about my being able to take charge of the paper began to fade. Once Dave read my article and saw that I was a capable writer, he began to see me differently.

Over the next few weeks, he began to get an ear for understanding me. He trained his ears to listen more intently when I spoke, and I, in turn, learned to speak more distinctly when I talked to him.

I got the first edition of the paper out that semester without overlooking any major stories — and without help or nudging from Nate. I had a new staff to help.

Over the long, lazy summer months, however, it seemed as if some of my writers also had grown indolent and forgotten some of the grammar rules. I got a letter after our first paper came out pointing out a slew of grammatical errors in the paper, particularly on the sports page.

I had become so engrossed with the news pages, I neglected to check on sports or even read the sports copy. I left the sports section completely up to Randal, unaware that he might need some help, too.

Now, I had to call the sports editor into my office. It was times like that when I wished I wasn't the boss. Randal was my friend. How could I rebuke a friend?

Still, I knew what I had to do, for the sake of the paper. I summoned Randal to my office and handed him the letter. He read it slowly, a look of gloom falling on his face. I told Randal I owed him an apology for not helping him more, but I made it clear that he was going to have to improve. Though, ultimately, I was responsible for all the paper, the sports page was his responsibility.

Like a puppy that had just been scolded by its master, Randal looked like he had lost his last friend. He apologized for slacking off and vowed to work harder. He asked if he could keep the letter and slowly walked out of the office.

It wasn't the first time that I had given a staff member a tongue-lashing or the first time I had gotten tough with

Randal. But I hated it more each time. Randal started as the sports editor soon after I took over as editor. In fact, one of my first decisions after taking over was to hire Randal.

He had a tough time that first semester, much as I did at first. Rick said I might have to let him go because he just didn't seem to be getting the hang of it. But I just couldn't fire Randal. He was a dedicated worker; he just needed a little coaxing. I decided to give Randal another chance.

I remembered those who gave me a second chance when I had failed, and I was grateful for another chance. Randal deserved a second chance, too. Now, I wondered if I had done the right thing.

Randal took the letter to heart. He took the letter and tacked it up on the wall next to his desk along with some baseball cards and a tethered magazine cover. I tried to help him all I could, and Dave began to work with him on his writing.

Soon, Randal began making great strides. Every now and again, when Randal was going through a tough time, I'd see him take down that letter and read it again. Then, he would stick it back on the wall next to the baseball cards and magazine cover and go back to work.

I was glad I had given Randal a second chance, just as I was glad when someone had given me another chance.

Weeks passed, and everything seemed to run smoothly. I was more organized than I was the previous year. I finally seemed to be taking charge of my destiny.

Life's Uncertainties

Each day brought new and exciting challenges for me. In October of that year, the university inaugurated its eighth president, and I was to cover the ceremony.

It was a huge celebration with great fanfare. Dignitaries from across the state attended the event. It was my first major writing assignment as editor, and everything had to be right. This paper marked an important day in the university's history.

I was prouder of that issue than any other. It received accolades from students and faculty alike. I received letters and phone calls from people commenting on the beautiful, full-color picture that dominated the front page that week.

It was a great time. Inside, though, my emotions were on a roller coaster. When times were good and things were running smooth, I was on top of the world, but when things weren't so good, I got depressed.

I was lonely again. My life seemed void without Nate there, the way it had been my first semester at West Texas. It seemed as though I had no one. I had friends, but they didn't include me in their activities. They made plans without any thought to me. It was as if I was invisible when it came to them.

I drowned myself in my work to keep my mind off my troubles. I would do anything to keep from returning to the destitute of those four walls back in my dorm room.

Problems started to crop up again at the paper. People were slacking off, and writers failed to turn in stories I had counted on to fill the paper. To me, the paper came first, and I didn't understand how people could be so negligent of their duties. What I failed to realize was that they had other priorities, with classes and homework.

I worked hard to put out a paper each week and thought everyone else should put forth that same effort. I felt that my staff had let me down. It wasn't that they didn't care. It was just that they still had lives outside of the paper.

As the weeks went by, things got progressively worse. Complaints began to filter in about the paper, and again I blamed myself. I thought everything was my fault. This time, instead of trying to keep my feelings bottled up inside, I decided to get help.

I thought I could do everything by myself, but I discovered I couldn't do it alone. I needed help. I decided to see a counselor, so I made an appointment with the disabled students' counselor.

My emotions were wracked when I showed up at the counseling center on campus. I told Kay about the loss I felt after Nate and Rick left, the rejection I felt when I was left out of activities and the insecurity I had about my position on the newspaper.

Kay was reassuring, her words consoling. She told me I was trying to overcompensate for my disability by working so feverishly, then blaming myself when things went wrong. No one is perfect; life is not without failures.

It helped to talk about my feelings. I poured out my heart to her, unloading years of guilt and frustrations.

No one could know I was seeing a counselor, not even my parents. They would think I was weak, so I went each week in secret. Kay helped me deal with the emotions I'd kept locked up inside me for years.

I had to deal with my feelings if I hoped to live a normal life. Others were beginning to notice my irrational response any time someone questioned me quite legitimately about my work. Dave, especially, had noticed the manner in which I reacted in our critique sessions.

While on the outside I accepted their criticism openly, on the inside I was burning with anger because I saw it as questioning my ability. I often left our critiques and went back to my office and started slamming things around like a wild man.

Kay reminded me how far I had come since those first days at West Texas when even the professors questioned my ability. Kay taught me to be honest when people hurt me by leaving me out, and she told me to ask others to go do something instead of waiting for them to ask me.

She told me that not everyone was going to share my passion for the paper. I couldn't expect people to give 100 percent of their efforts to the paper all of the time. But she told me to tell people when they let me down.

I got a lot out of our talks, and I began to work through my feelings of insecurity. I saw that in their criticism, they were only trying to help me become a better writer and editor. My relationships with my friends also improved as I became bolder in asking them to go places.

As the days ticked down toward graduation, I faced still another problem: getting and keeping a job. My years at West Texas were the best years of my life, but they were quickly coming to an end and soon I would have to face the real world. My bitter disappointment over not getting an internship had made me lose hope over my chances of landing a job after graduation.

I began to think I had wasted five years of college only to return home after graduation to do nothing for the rest of my life. Dave was painfully honest about my chances of getting a job. He knew from experience after having worked in the fast-paced business for many years and hiring young reporters that my chances of landing a job as a reporter were slim.

He said if I hoped to find a job, I had to concentrate on larger newspapers where I could work on a desk editing copy, rather than pounding the payment trying to get a story.

Dave did everything he could to help in the job search. He called several editors at metropolitan newspapers, hoping they could help. Finally, he convinced his wife, who was the executive editor of the Amarillo newspaper, to give me another chance at taking the job test that I failed two years before. He even drove me to the interview.

But it was to no avail. I failed the test again and when a job came up they offered it to someone who scored higher on the test.

Still, I wouldn't be dissuaded. I sent letters to every small-town newspaper in the area, hoping they would have something. Meanwhile, graduation was rapidly approaching.

The week before I left school for the final time, I heard about a job for a reporter on the newspaper back home. My spirits soared. Although my parents warned me not to get my hopes up, I knew this job had to be for me. The timing was perfect. It had to be God's plan. I always believed that God would have something for me when I graduated.

I finished my last test and rushed back to Pampa. I was so excited. Everything was falling into place, or so I thought. I wasted no time after I returned home in going to the news office to apply for the job. I took my resume and copies of my writing, confident that they would hire me on the spot.

The editor took my application and told me he would let me know his decision in a week or two. I wasn't worried. I'll get the job, I kept telling myself. God will provide a way.

I really believed I would get the job, and I could go to graduation without worrying about the future.

It was an emotional day as Mom and Dad took me to the graduation ceremony. The whole family turned out — Karen, Grandma Altman, Grandpa, aunts and uncles. It was an emotional day as I walked across the stage and graduated with honors.

It was a proud moment, one many people thought would never happen. It had been a struggle, both emotionally and physically, but it was all worth it now. All the pain and sorrow, all the heartaches — it had all been worth it when I received my diploma.

I left West Texas State University stronger than when I came. What I learned couldn't be taught in any classroom. What I learned came only through many trials and sorrows, tears and joy. I learned that to get anything in life, you have to make it happen. The road is not an easy one, but perseverance will see you through. I thanked God for leading me along the long and often tenebrous journey.

After all the celebrations of graduation, I sat back and waited for the call from *The Pampa News*. Two weeks past, then three, and I had heard nothing from the newspaper. They hadn't called me for an interview or to offer me a job. Finally, after a month, I called the editor to see if they had filled the job. He assured me they were still reviewing my application and would make a decision within the week.

Meanwhile, I had received responses from the letters I mailed out to the smaller papers. One by one, they turned me down. Either there were no openings or they were looking for someone with more experience. I was beginning to doubt.

Dave, still determined to help me find a job, called me every week. He told me not to give up. "It takes time. Something will turn up," he said.

At last, a letter came in the mail from *The Pampa News*. My heart pounding, I tore open the envelope, hoping . . . praying that it would hold the key to my future. I got a big disappointment. I had been rejected again. They had hired someone else for the job.

Believing

I was beginning to lose all hope of ever getting a job. Still, I believed.

Out of desperation, I went to see the job counselor at the Texas Rehabilitation Commission. He had told me to come see him after graduation, and he would try to help me find a job. But now, after losing all chance of working at my hometown newspaper, my chances of finding work looked bleak.

Mr. Howell didn't hold out much hope of finding me a job any time soon. He warned me that it could take a year or more to find work. People just weren't willing to take a chance on someone with a disability as severe as mine.

Since another job wasn't likely at the paper any time soon, Mr. Howell said I might have to try another line of work. He suggested that I look to companies hiring someone for public relations, where I still could use my writing. But I had my heart set on working at a newspaper.

I left Mr. Howell's office discouraged and heartbroken. Dad tried to boost my spirits. "It's only been a month," he said in the car on the way home. "You have plenty of time." But he was beginning to doubt, too.

If I had taken Mr. Howell's advice, I would have sat around and done nothing, but I wasn't going to give up. I wrote to the Texas Press Association, asking that my name be included in a weekly listing of job applicants. Editors from around the state would see it. I saw it as my last chance.

At church the next week, my Sunday school teacher prayed with me. He was a man of great faith. He believed God already had a job prepared for me. He prayed and asked God to show me his will.

Then, he told me just to believe and to expect an answer that week. He encouraged me to keep the faith. My spirits soared. I believed God heard those prayers.

The next day, I received a call from an editor on the Texas coast. She had seen my name in the Texas Press Association's listings. Unfortunately, the job was for a reporter and photographer and meant I would have to leave my family and move hundreds of miles away from home.

I would have done anything for a job, but I knew this wasn't the job for me. God had something better for me. I thanked the editor but declined her offer for an interview. I kept praying that God would show me his will.

I got three other calls in the next two days, all from editors who had seen my listing. But they all wanted reporters, and I had resigned myself to finding a job as a copy editor as Dave advised.

Finally, the call came. On Thursday of that week, I was laying in bed when the phone rang. My heart skipped a beat every time the phone rang, hoping for a call from someone who had seen my listing. Dad answered it from the front of the house and summoned me to the phone.

It was Dave's wife, Cathy Martindale, with the *Amarillo Globe-News*.

"Are you enjoying your summer?" she asked.

"Yes," I replied.

"Are you ready for it to end?"

"Very much!" I said, anticipating her next question.

She offered me a job as a copy editor. She said she liked my work from the beginning, but there was still the matter of the editing test. Twice I had taken the test, and twice I had failed. When a job came up earlier that spring, she had to hire someone who scored higher on the test.

Now, there was another job. She realized that one score on one test wasn't a true test of a person's ability. She had watched my progress over the last year on the college paper, and with a good word from Dave, she decided to give me a chance.

I don't remember what she said beyond that. I was too excited. I could hardly answer her questions.

When I hung up the phone, I could hardly speak. I was overcome with joy. "Calm down and tell me what she said," Dad said.

Tears of joy flooded our house that day. I was 24 years old when I got my first job. It was a day I never thought would come. After coming home from college and learning about the job at my hometown paper, I believed that job was meant for me. When I didn't get the job, I became angry and bitter.

I couldn't understand why God would allow that to happen. Why would a job open up at that exact time if God didn't intend it for me?

I didn't have the faith to see God had something better for my life. Now, I realize that God did have something better for me. He allowed me to go through that rejection to show me I had to trust him in everything.

Suddenly, my life was thrown into a whirlwind. With less than two weeks until I started work, there was much to be decided.

Mom and Dad accepted my leaving the nest better than I expected. After living away at school for three years, they realized that with a little help I could make it on my own. I finally had grown up in my parents' eyes.

When Mom started talking about finding me an apartment and buying furniture, it frightened me. What if I can't do the job? What if I fail? I suggested that I rent a room at the YMCA for a week or two until I saw if I could handle it. I was so afraid I was going to fail.

Mom made calls around town, but none of the places that rented rooms by the week seemed suited to accommodate someone with a disability like mine. Once again, God intervened. Mom heard about an apartment complex for people with disabilities. There, I could test the waters in my quest for independence.

That Saturday afternoon, Mom and Dad drove me to Amarillo to inspect the building. The apartments were in an older neighborhood, just off the downtown district. It was near enough the newspaper office that I could ride my bike to work in all kinds of weather.

Each apartment had two large bedrooms, a spacious kitchen and an accessible bathroom. It was more room than I needed, but it was a bargain at $250 a month.

A retired man and his wife lived on the grounds to help the tenants adjust to living on their own, though their goal was to see that the tenants got along without their help.

Mom was disappointed when the man told us that I could only stay there temporarily. Then, I'd have to move on and let someone else come in who needed the help. Mom was hoping I could live there permanently. I was just glad to have a place to go.

With my living arrangements settled, I could concentrate fully on my job. I started work on the copy desk the following week, working side by side with other editors. I knew this job was made for me, and I was ready to plunge head long into my work.

Everyone made me feel welcome. No one appeared conscious of my handicap or upset by it. I was more conscious of it than anybody. I was so eager to do a good job.

I was given the same responsibilities as any other beginning copy editor, which wasn't much at first. I spent the first week training. I learned more in a week than in three years of school, or so it seemed.

In the newspaper business, timing is everything. There was no time to muse and mull, and with my rudimentary typing skills, I was slower than the other copy editors. It took me twice as long to edit stories. Still, I concentrated on the job at hand and didn't budge until it was finished.

After the first week, I was moved to the night shift, working on the morning edition. I continued to work closely with the assistant managing editor. He checked my work before the stories went into the paper, and at the end of each day, he gave me a critique of my work, to tell me if I overlooked any crucial errors or wrote any inaccurate headlines. He was very helpful and encouraging in those first few days.

In spite of my fears, I became more skilled in editing. I learned more every day, but it still wasn't enough to reassure me. I needed constant reassurance that my work was satisfactory. I prayed each night that God would help me keep my job.

Everyone assured me that I was progressing. Still, I worried. If I didn't get praise from the copy chief, I thought something was wrong. I knew there was no such thing as a perfect paper, but I became upset over the slightest criticism or any time anybody pointed out a mistake.

But it was gratifying each time I caught a mistake, and when the papers rolled off the press, I knew that I had a part in it. It was hard work and long hours, but it fulfilled a longing in my life — a longing to work and live a productive life.

It was well after midnight when I finished work, which meant I had to ride home in the dark. The streets were well lighted. My route was along the downtown district of mostly businesses and small shops. The streets were deserted when I came along. There wasn't a soul in sight, except when I had to pass a couple of nightclubs.

I usually came along about the time the bars were closing, and everyone was heading home. Mom worried about me being out at that time of night. "Why don't you call a cab?" she badgered me. But I didn't want to spend my hard-earned money on cab fare.

Besides, no one will bother me, I assured her. Still, it was a little unnerving. I stared straight ahead, without veering to the right or the left, and pedaled as fast as I could. I didn't slow down for anything. I kept moving and praying that God's hedge of protection would be around me. No one ever tried to harm me.

When the weather started turning cold, I reluctantly accepted rides with the other copy editors. They took turns picking me up and taking me home from work. They were kind and said they didn't mind, but I didn't want to be a burden. I wanted to make my own way.

On My Own

Each day was a learning experience. Not only did I have to learn to do laundry and keep house, I also had to learn to cook.

I was a culinary disaster. I even burned toast. Mom kept me stocked with a supply of homemade, frozen dinners. Whenever she cooked a big meal, she always made a little extra and tucked it away in the freezer for me.

I was afraid to use the electric range. I was afraid the grease would splash out and burn me, but after weeks of fast-food restaurants and frozen dinners, I was starving for some home-cooked food. I decided to try to cook. My first meal was hamburger casserole.

The directions seemed simple enough. I can do it, I assured myself. I got the old, battered skillet that Mom had used to prepare so many meals with hands of love and started browning the meat.

I had the heat too high, and it started burning. Then, when I went to pour in the macaroni, the pan was too small and it began spilling over the sides. I poured more on the floor than in the pan.

It was edible, but not nearly as good as the meals Mom made. After that, I limited my cooking to TV dinners. I ate out some, but there weren't many restaurants within riding distance.

Going anywhere in Amarillo was a struggle. Unlike at school where everything was at my feet, Amarillo was spread out. I rode my bike when I could, but most places were just too far. The nearest grocery store was three miles away.

Once a week, the apartment manager graciously offered to take anyone who needed a ride to the market. One by one, he would haul us to the store to buy groceries. I was grateful for the ride, but I wanted to go on my own. Trouble was, everything was so far.

It took me all day to go anywhere. One day, I decided to go shopping for some new clothes. Now that I had a job, I had to look nice.

I got up one morning and headed out to the mall. I was sure I could get home in plenty of time before I had to be at work. I started out the door and down to the corner bus stop.

I was so proud of myself for being so independent. For the first time in my life, I had financial independence. I was earning my own money. I got $350 a week, which was more money than I had ever seen. The night I got my first check, the other editors invited me to go out for a drink after work. I couldn't say no. I was so thrilled they asked me that I went, even though I knew it was wrong to squander my money on drinking. Still, I wanted so desperately to fit in and make friends.

I was careful with my money and tried to save, but I couldn't help but going on shopping sprees, buying furniture more suited for my new apartment. And I had to buy new clothes. The clothes I wore to school didn't seem suitable anymore.

The bus took me downtown, where I had to get off and wait for another bus to take me across town to the mall. I sat down on a bench so I would see when my bus arrived. Finally, I saw a big, blue bus round the corner and stop at the corner. I got up and started toward the bus. In the meantime, another one had pulled up behind it, then another and another. I didn't know which one was the right one. I asked one of the drivers which bus went to the mall.

He pointed to the first one. "But you better hurry. It's getting ready to pull out," he said.

I ran to catch it, but it was too late. The doors slammed shut, and it took off without me. I had to wait 30 minutes for another one.

It was past noon when I arrived at the mall. I was starving. All that waiting had made me hungry. I decided to get something to eat before I started my shopping. Everyone else must have had the same idea. The food court was packed for the noon rush. I stood in line nearly half an hour before I got to order. I finally got my food and sat down to eat.

I felt better once I had eaten. At last, I was ready to shop. I made my way down the long hall, dashing in and out of stores until I found clothes I liked. I found a pair of brown dress slacks and a pullover shirt.

"What size do you wear?" the man behind the counter asked.

I thought for a minute. I didn't know what size I wore. Mom had always bought my clothes for me. "I think I wear a large. I'm not sure."

"Maybe you better try them on," he said, sounding a little irritated.

The man showed me to the dressing room and handed me the pants. I went into the cramped room and started to change. There was hardly any room to move around. I scrambled around to take off my pants, then started to put on the new pair. I got them on and stepped from behind the curtain to look in the mirror.

The pants were too big. They swallowed me up. The clerk quickly brought another pair and sent me back into the tiny changing room. This time, they were a fit.

"I'll take them," I said boastfully.

I bought a whole new outfit, right down to socks and underwear. I was having fun trying on clothes when I glanced at my watch. It was 3 o'clock. I had to be at work in an hour. I quickly finished paying for my purchases and rushed outside where the bus let me out.

The bus was just rounding the corner when I came out. I quickly boarded the bus and headed home. When I got back to my apartment, my ride was waiting to take me to work. I didn't even have time to change. I just had to get in the car and go. I was exhausted, but I was proud. I had made my own decisions.

A Deeper Walk

As soon as I got settled in my new apartment, I began going to church. The church was too far for me to ride my bike, so the youth pastor, Roger, and his wife came and picked me up. I had met Roger and Laurie at college. They came and ministered to the college students each week at a Bible study on campus.

They were about the only people I knew when I came to Amarillo, so when I began looking for a church, I called them. They graciously offered to pick me up each Sunday.

I often had to work on Sunday, but I went to church every chance I got. It became a place of refuge. I felt such a peace there. The people were warm and caring and welcomed me into the congregation.

The people of First Assembly of God were a people of faith. They believed in miracles. One Sunday not long after I started going there, I received a word of knowledge. I had been praying at the altar when a man came over and told me God was going to heal me. He prayed for me and told me to believe God for a miracle.

I always had believed in God's power to heal me. Now, I believed it even more. I prayed for days afterward that God would help me to have enough faith to receive my healing.

I wasn't healed that week, or that year. I didn't understand why I wasn't healed right then. I felt that my faith must be too weak, that it wasn't strong enough to receive God's touch.

I simply couldn't understand why. Why didn't God do what he said he would do? I struggled with my faith a great deal that year, especially when that word was given to me again a few months later. I felt God had to heal me then.

When it didn't come when I thought it should, I became angry. I turned from God. I rebelled. I still prayed. I still went to church. But I wasn't living the way God wanted me to live.

I thought if I wasn't healed, I couldn't do anything for God. He began to show me that even if he didn't heal me right then, he could use me just as I was. He had a purpose and a time for everything. I had to keep believing. I had to hold onto my faith.

The church became like a second family to me. They prayed diligently for me and encouraged me to remain faithful in my walk with God.

I felt God was beginning to stir me, calling me into a deeper relationship with him. I was trying to it on my own, without leaning on him. He wanted me to turn everything over to him and trust him. I had to learn to surrender my will to him, which meant giving up some things in my life. When I did, my faith grew.

The first few months were lonely. At least at school there were other people around. In my apartment, it was so quiet I almost went insane. I lay in bed at night listening to the thunderous silence. I had accepted being alone. I even liked the solitude sometimes, but I missed my family. Holidays were the worst. Thanksgiving came, and I had planned to go to Pampa for the holiday. Dad was going to come get me and take me back for a big family feast. The night before Thanksgiving, there was a big snowstorm, and Dad couldn't get through. I was stranded in Amarillo.

I was disappointed, of course, but I had to make the most of it. For Thanksgiving dinner, I rode two blocks through the icy streets and below-freezing temperatures to the senior citizens center. There, I saw a lot of other lonely people and shared a hot meal.

Even though I was the youngest one there, the people were kind and made me feel welcome. I had a hot meal and time to think about how fortunate I was.

I had much to be thankful for. I had a job, a new apartment, and I was seeing my dream come true. I thought about all that God had given me that year. I was truly blessed.

When Christmas rolled around, I had to work and again had to stay in Amarillo. Being the new kid, I had to work all the holidays. I didn't mind though. I was just thankful to have a job.

The new year started well. My supervisors seemed pleased with my progress. My speed increased, and I was less conscious of my disability. I still strived for perfection, but when I made a mistake — and they did happen — I didn't become angry over it. I tried to learn from my mistakes and move forward.

Dream Come True

There was, however, one dream left unfulfilled. One goal I hadn't reached. I wanted to drive a car. It was the one thing that stood between me and true independence.

I had depended on others to take me everywhere. I depended on people to take me to work, people to take me shopping. It was like riding in the wheelchair when I started junior high school. It was easier, but I had to depend on others to take me where I wanted to go, and I desperately wanted to stand on my own.

I never lost hope that someday I would drive. Ever since I was 16 and my parents dashed my hopes of getting a license, I set my sights on driving. It was a dream I held in my heart.

More and more, I felt like I was missing out on part of life by not being able to get out more. One cold, wintry night, I had planned to go to a concert. I bought my ticket weeks ahead because the show was sure to be a sellout. I had looked forward to that night for weeks.

A friend from work promised to take me, but she became ill at the last minute and couldn't go. The civic center was only about a mile from my apartment. I easily could've ridden my bicycle. I had ridden farther plenty of times, but it was the dead of winter and freezing outside.

Determined that nothing was going to keep me from the concert, I did the thing I had scoffed at when Mom suggested it. I called a cab. Afraid that I wouldn't be able to find a telephone after the show, I asked the driver to pick me up promptly at 10. Surely the show will be over by then, I thought. I might miss the last few minutes of the show, but I wanted to beat the crowd out of the coliseum.

The coliseum was packed, and the country band shook the house. The floor vibrated beneath me. The crowd was pumped, but the whole time, I kept looking at my watch. I was afraid I would miss my ride.

It was 9:30 when the opening act left the stage. I waited patiently, hoping to see a little of the headline act before I had to catch my ride, but by the time they set up the stage for the featured band, it was a quarter until 10. I was going to miss the rest of the show.

As the band took the stage, I began to make my way out of the coliseum. I was crushed. I had waited so long for that night, and now I was going to miss most of the concert. I could hear the music echoing through the hall as I left.

On the way home that night, I made up my mind. I was going to get my driver's license. I was never going to miss out on anything again.

When I told my parents of my plans to get my license, they were skeptical. They still wondered if I'd be able to handle driving, but they had to let me stand on my own. I was an adult now, and they realized I was going to do it with or without their blessing.

My parents surprised me. They didn't try to discourage me from trying to get my license. They realized if I was going to live in Amarillo, I needed a car. It had become increasingly harder for me to get around in the city.

Dad came over and took me to the Department of Public Safety to see about my chances of getting a license. Dad told the DPS trooper his fears about letting me drive when I was 16. The trooper shared Dad's concerns that my reflexes wouldn't be quick enough to make sudden stops.

The road officer knew about cerebral palsy. He had been through this situation before. His daughter suffered from the crippling disease. The trooper said his daughter probably would never be able to drive, and he didn't feel I could either.

I was furious. "Don't judge me by your daughter," I wanted to scream. "I'm not your daughter. Give me a chance to see what *I* can do."

The trooper saw that I wasn't going to be dissuaded. He reluctantly agreed to let me take the written test and get a learner's permit. Then, after I practiced driving on the road, I could take a road test. If I passed, I would get my license.

Dad warned me not to get my hopes up. I might not pass, but I was overjoyed. All I wanted was a chance to try. I got a driving manual and studied it day and night. After only two weeks, I had worn the cover off the book, and I knew every rule of the road. I was ready to take the written test.

There was no doubt in my mind that I would pass. The real test would come when I got behind the wheel. What if Dad was right? Maybe my reflexes wouldn't be swift enough. But I had to try. I had to know.

I passed the written test with ease. The trooper smiled as he handed me my learner's permit, but I could see he still had doubts. "You still have to pass the road test," he said.

I left that day more confident than ever that I would drive a car.

I was ready to climb behind the wheel right then and start driving, but Dad stopped me. "Wait a minute. You're going to need a lot of practice before you're ready to drive in town," he said. "When you come home on weekends, you can practice. Maybe in a year or so you'll be ready."

A year! My heart fell on the floor. I couldn't wait a year. I was ready now. But with Dad 60 miles away, I had little chance to practice.

The thought of having to wait another year was almost more than I could bear. That night after Dad left, the answer hit me. I would take driving lessons. I would get someone to teach me to drive.

Early the next morning, I set out on my bike for the driving school. I was exhausted and out of breath by the time I reached the school. I could hardly speak from riding so hard.

The driving instructor didn't seem concerned about my handicap. He had worked with people who had been injured in accidents, teaching them to drive again. He was sure he could teach me. He asked me a few questions, then he scheduled my first lesson. For $30 a hour, he would teach me to drive.

Two days later, the instructor picked me up for my first lesson. I was nervous and excited all rolled into one. I squirmed in the seat as I strained to fasten the seat belt and adjust the rear-view mirror.

I thought the instructor might have doubts about teaching me to drive if he saw me having difficulty with the seat belt, but he told me not to worry.

"Take your time," he said. "It doesn't matter if it takes you longer to fasten your seat belt. The real test is how you do once you get on the road."

Finally, I got strapped in and pulled away from the curb and into traffic. I was on my way. I didn't seem to make the man nervous as I did when I had Mom or Dad in the car with me. The instructor guided me through a maze of streets, weaving in and out of traffic, changing lanes and turning.

I drove to the newspaper office and practiced parking in front of the building. Several of my co-workers past by while I was pulling away. They looked as if they had seen a ghost. They were shocked to see me behind the wheel. I waved and smiled proudly as I pulled away.

I drove for nearly an hour. When I pulled up in front of my apartment, the instructor commended me. "Who said you couldn't drive?" he asked.

I told him what the trooper said about my reflexes.

"You handled this car like you've been driving all your life," he said. "But if you'd like, I can talk to the trooper for you."

"You don't think I'll have trouble passing the test?" I asked.

"Not at all."

My hopes soared. It really was going to happen. I was going to get my license! I took two more lessons. The instructor showed me how to parallel park and told me what to expect on the road test. Finally, after only three lessons, the driving instructor said, "You're ready for the test."

I wasn't sure I was ready. After all, it had only been a month, but the instructor convinced me to take the test.

A few days before Christmas, Dad drove me back to the DPS office. I thought I would be nervous before the test, but I was strangely calm. The trooper got into the car and instructed me to pull forward and parallel park.

This was the one thing I had trouble with. I thought about how the driving instructor had demonstrated it just weeks before. I slipped into the spot like a hand in a glove.

The examiner was shocked. She sat beside me scribbling notes on a pad as she directed me through a maze of maneuvers. I proceeded cautiously through each intersection, held my breath at each turn and prayed each time I came to a stop.

Finally, I pulled up in front of the office and waited as the trooper tallied my score. It was the longest three minutes of my life. She checked the score twice to be sure, then she said, "Congratulations. You passed."

I couldn't believe it. I raced inside where Dad was pacing nervously. "I passed! I GOT MY LICENSE!" I screamed. Dad was a little surprised. I don't think he really expected me to pass. Not on the first try anyway. But he was thrilled and proud of me.

I wanted to rush out and buy a car after I got my license. Any car. I had waited nearly 10 years for that day, and I was ready to plunk down my money on the first car I laid eyes on.

"You don't want to make a decision you'll regret," Dad said. He promised to come back the next weekend and help me shop for a car.

My parents were afraid I was going to run out and buy a car before they had a chance to get back. "Don't do anything without telling us," they said.

In the meantime, Dad did some checking. My Uncle John was a car dealer down state. Dad called him to see if he had any used cars that would fit my needs. My aunt and uncle were so thrilled about me getting my license, they made me a deal I couldn't refuse.

Uncle John made me a deal on a Chevolet Cavilier. It had had some work done on it, but it was still in mint condition. When Mom called to tell me about it, I was so excited I was willing to take it sight unseen. All I wanted to know was, "When can we go pick it up?"

Mom and Dad drove down to pick up the car on New Year's Eve. I had to work, so I didn't even see the car before they got it. It didn't matter, though. I was so thrilled that I didn't care what it looked like. I just wanted a car.

At work that weekend, that was all I could talk about. I could hardly wait until Mom and Dad got back with the car. Everyone assumed I would need special equipment on the car. They were surprised when I told them I didn't need any modifications. Everyone was thrilled for me — mostly because they would no longer have to chauffeur me around — but they were genuinely happy for me.

Finally, after walking on clouds all weekend, I heard Mom and Dad pull up behind my apartment. I was so excited. I ran outside to greet them. I kept walking around the car, my face brimming with pride. "Awesome," I said again and again. "It's awesome." It was white with a red strip down the side.

I wanted to jump in and take off. But I couldn't. Not yet. There was one hurdle I hadn't counted on — one that almost kept me off the road permanently. Insurance. I was a high risk, and no one wanted to take a chance on me.

The man at the insurance office was frank in telling me that because of my disability, it was going to be hard to sell me to the insurance company. The policy would cost more, too.

I was angry. I thought he was trying to swindle me. I was sure he was taking advantage of me because I was handicapped.

To make matters worse, I couldn't even drive the car until the insurance company approved my application, and that would take several days. I had to leave the car sitting in my parents' driveway and go back to Amarillo while I waited to see if the company would accept me.

I was crushed. I had bragged to everyone at work that I would be driving to work when I came back. I went so far as to tell them not to pick me up anymore. I was so sure I would have a car when I went back.

I was heartbroken when I had to call them back and ask them if they could pick me up awhile longer.

The insurance agent assured me it would take only a few days to process the paperwork and I would get a letter in the mail. What's three or four days, I thought. I had waited 10 years, but those days were the longest three days of my life.

Each day, I rushed out to the mailbox hoping to find a letter. When it didn't come, I flew into a tantrum. I became angry and kicked my bicycle in fits of rage. A week passed, and the papers still hadn't arrived. I called Mom every day, yelling and screaming. I demanded that she call the agent and find out what was going on. I was convinced he was trying to hustle me, and I wasn't going to be cheated.

The agent assured Mom the papers were in the mail. Two more days passed, and I didn't get the papers. I grew more incensed each day. Finally, the agent got tired of dealing with me. He issued me a temporary card so I could at least drive the car. I didn't understand why he didn't do that from the beginning, but at least now I could drive the car.

When Mom and Dad brought my car to me later that evening, my anger turned to jubilation. I was on top of the world.

After my parents left, I just sat in my car reveling over my latest achievement. That night, I cruised through the neighborhood, driving up and down the streets. I felt like I had been released from captivity. At last, I was free.

New Day Dawning

Soon after I got my license, I started working the day shift at the paper. It was a welcome change from working nights and the long hours, and I had more time to go out in my new car in the evenings.

I worked with three young women on the copy desk — Beth, Laura and Larri Jo — along with Bruce, the assistant city editor, and Raenell, the desk clerk. There was also a sports copy editor, Greg, in the early-morning crew. Everyone made me feel welcome. They made me feel like I was a part of the team, and I came to count them as some of my best friends.

Before, I always had felt like an intruder. Everyone was nice enough, but I really didn't fit in. It was different working with the Missies, as the three girls were known around the newsroom. They made me feel like I was part of them. They included me in their morning runs to the bagel shop and sometimes invited me to go out with them after work. I finally felt like I belonged.

We rotated jobs on the copy desk, and I was expected to take a turn at all the jobs, even the ones I didn't particularly enjoy.

They didn't pity me. They treated me the same as everyone else, which was how I wanted to be treated but how many were afraid to treat me.

It was still lonely sometimes, but now that I had a car I became more outgoing. I went out more, even if I had to go alone. I went to movies or just drove around. Anything was better than sitting and staring at those four walls.

In my search for company, I joined a disabled advocacy group. The Panhandle Action Center for Independent Living was a welcome refuge. They had classes to help people with disabilities find jobs, budget their money and take care of themselves. There were also social activities, which was the reason I went.

I thought it would be easier making friends among the people who came to the center. Most were like me. Many had disabilities; others just needed a helping hand until they got back on their feet, but we all shared a common goal. We strived for independence.

I thought they would be more tolerant of someone with a disability. I was sure they would accept one of their own and that I would make friends in no time.

But I didn't find the one thing that I was desperately longing for — a true friend, the kind of friend I had found in Nate. I continued to struggle with communicating with others. I knew if I wanted to make friends, I had to be a friend. I had to open up and share with others — something I just couldn't make myself do.

I met a lot of new people at the center. I even met up with the girl that I had rode to camp with years before,

Alisa Burns. She was all grown up now and quite different from the young girl I met at the Lions Club camp when I was a boy.

I had seen her at the center but hadn't really talked to her until one night I saw her at a singles dance. Neither of us danced, but we had a good time reliving our days at camp.

A lot had changed in the years since we'd seen each other. Alisa left home when she was 16. She moved to Amarillo after high school. She worked when she could find it and took classes at the community college. It was a struggle for her just to get around some days, but she made it. Like me, she depended on God's goodness to provide a way.

We started going out and quickly became close friends. We had many of the same struggles and shared many of the same beliefs, mainly about God.

It helped having someone to talk to. It gave me hope in a world of isolation. I felt a special closeness with Alisa. I understood her struggles, and she understood mine. I could tell her things no one else could understand. I had never met anyone like her.

We dated for nearly two years, and I thought I had found the right girl for me. We even planned to get married. I never thought I would ever get married, but Alisa had given me something no one else could — true companionship.

A few months before we were to be married, something happened. It was as if God showed us a mirror of our future lives, and they didn't match. Like me, Alisa had dreams. She had dreams of being a missionary and sharing God's love with others. She also wanted children, something I wasn't sure I wanted in my life.

When we went our separate ways to pursue different dreams, I was devastated. Alisa would always hold a special place in my heart. I knew I had to let go, and I had to look ahead, too.

The loneliness returned, and troubles began to flood my life like waves. I was unhappy at work. My life seemed to have no meaning. I was depressed. I wanted to run away. I thought if I could get a job in another place, if I could move away from Amarillo, that the troubles would disappear.

But that wasn't the answer. Instead of running away, I needed to run to God. And when I ran to him, I felt him put his loving arms around me. God began to teach me a lesson — that he loved me and would always be with me.

I knew God had a reason for me to be where I was. God had a plan. He was also teaching me to be content with what I had.

All my life, I always felt if I could just have something else, I would be happy. When I was young, I thought if I just got healed, I'd be happy. Later, I said if I had a good job, I'd be satisfied. Then, I thought if had a better job, I'd never want anything else. But the truth was that I would never be satisfied.

It's all right to have goals and dreams, but somewhere along the way I had to accept what I have and be happy with that.

I had to learn to be content with my station in life — whatever that station is. God knows my deepest hopes and dreams, and he has a plan for my life that is better than anything I could hope for. I just had to let go and trust him.

I didn't know if I would ever find the right girl and settle down. I didn't know if I would be healed. But I believed in God, and I began to live life one day at a time, looking to God to satisfy me rather than earthly things.

Like a child being led by the hand, I knew God was directing my path. I knew that he knew the plans for my life, and I only had to look to him. In his timing, he would reveal his perfect plan for my life.

I continued to struggle with the unanswered questions. I continued to have doubts, uncertain of what the future might bring. I had many unexplored dreams and hopes still before me, but I knew that through the eyes of faith, all the obstacles would be removed. And all I had to do was believe.

Epilogue

∞

If you put your faith in Jesus Christ, you have the promise of eternal life. You can find hope in him, just as I did. God desires to give us the desires of our heart.

Yet, until we recognize our need and put our faith in him, sin separates us from his promises. "For all have sinned and fall short of the glory of God and are justified freely by his grace through the redemption that came by Christ Jesus" (Romans 3:23-24).

We must first confess our sins and acknowledge that without him, we have no hope for eternal life. "If we confess our sin, he is faithful and just and will forgive us our sins and purify us from all unrighteousness" (1 John 1:8-9).

Then, we must put our faith in Jesus Christ and invite him to be our personal savior. "Yet to all who received him, to those who believed in his name, he gave the right to become children of God" (John 1:12).

Faith is trusting in God to help us become who he wants us to be. Once we accept Christ as savior, his spirit takes root in our hearts.

It is the spirit of God that will lead and direct us, and it is only through faith that his spirit dwells in us. "For it is by grace you have been saved, through faith — and this not from yourselves, it is the gift of God — not by works, so that no one can boast" (Ephesians 2:8-9).

Through faith and a relationship with Jesus Christ, I overcame adversity. Without him, I could do nothing. If you have not accepted Jesus and put your faith in him, I invite you to say this simple prayer and ask him to come into your life:

> "Dear Jesus, I need you. I believe you died on the cross for my sins. Forgive my sins and come into my life. I put my faith in you and receive you as my savior. Thank you for dying for me and giving me eternal life. Help me to see with eyes of faith to become the person you want me to be. Amen."

To order additional copies of:

Through Eyes of Faith

send $12.99 plus $4.95 shipping and handling to:

Books, Etc.
PO Box 1406
Mukilteo, WA 98275

or have your credit card ready and call:

(800) 917-BOOK